Personal Reflections on Henri

Nouwen Then

Edited by
Christopher de Vinck

ZondervanPublishingHouse
Grand Rapids, Michigan

A Division of HarperCollinsPublishers

Nouwen Then
Copyright © 1999 by Christopher de Vinck
Requests for information should be addressed to:
📖 ZondervanPublishingHouse
Grand Rapids, Michigan 49530

Library of Congress Cataloging-in-Publication Data
de Vinck, Christopher.
    Nouwen then : personal reflections on Henri / edited by
Christopher de Vinck.
        p.   cm.
        ISBN 0-310-22462-4
        1. Nouwen, Henri J.M.   I. De Vinck, Christopher, 1951– .
BX4705.N87N87 1999
282'.092—dc21   99-18862
[B]   CIP

This edition printed on acid-free paper and meets the American National Standards Institute Z39.48 standard.

Interior design by Sherri L. Hoffman
Printed in the United States of America
99 00 01 02 03 04 05 /❖ DC/ 10 9 8 7 6 5 4 3 2 1

To Roe

My Partner in the Journey

Contents

Introduction

I'VE just returned from a difficult weekend. I was invited by an advocacy group to give a talk based on my books. The nonprofit organization's mission is to connect people to people. "Chris, there are people in nursing homes who are victims of accidents, once healthy people who now endure severe brain damage and will be in bed for the rest of their lives. They are incapable of talking, incapable of eating without a tube in their stomachs, and who are alone, abandoned by their families. We extend an invitation to anyone who would like to befriend these helpless, forgotten people in deep need of love."

Before my talk I had lunch with a reporter who quickly shared the sadness of the divorce she recently endured. "My husband was having an affair with his high school sweetheart since the first months of our twelve years of marriage. I came from a broken home. My father was an alcoholic. I wanted my marriage to work. When my husband said that this woman was just his friend, I believed him. I was naive. When I found out, and when I said I wanted a divorce, he blamed *me* for destroying the family, asking why I couldn't accept him as he was. He wanted to have me and the kids as a family, but he also wanted his girlfriend, and he called me the guilty one."

As I was signing books, a woman stepped up to the table and said that her nineteen-year-old son died last year on the basketball court from massive heart failure.

After the book signing, I was invited to a nursing home to visit people who had sustained traumatic brain damage. One patient was in his early thirties. When he was seventeen he sustained brain and physical damage when the motorcycle he was driving slipped out of

9

control. For sixteen years he has been in a bed. One eye is crooked and covered with a gray film; the other is straight. His body is rigid. His feet are stiff. His toes are curled. He drools. He has no one.

In the hotel room that night I was flipping through the channels on the television when I came upon HBO. We do not subscribe to this channel at home, and I'd heard a great deal about it, so I adjusted the hotel television and watched the program in progress. It was called *Autopsy*. This was a story about a young couple who married. There was a video film of the bride and groom dancing at their wedding. It turns out the woman, from almost the first days of the marriage, was slowly poisoning her new husband to death because she wanted to inherit his money.

The program continued, showing the coffin of the husband being exhumed after three years. The television flickered, and there was the actual decomposing body of the young man who died. The program kept switching back and forth between the couple dancing on the floor and the decomposed corpse on a table in a hospital.

Death, divorce, brain damage, loneliness, illness, murder.

It is raining outside as I write. The rhododendron leaves are smooth and glistening with their new coat of water. Two years ago today, September 21, 1996, Henri Nouwen died. An Airborne Express truck pulled up in front of the house, and I looked out the window as the driver stepped from the truck and walked to the front door. Before he could ring the doorbell, I opened the door and smiled. He smiled too as he handed me an eight-by-ten envelope. I said, "Thank you." He said, "You're welcome." I walked back into the house, sat on the living room couch, and pulled the tab of the envelope. The letter was from my editor. "We're excited about the release of your book, *Nouwen Then*. Enclosed is the art director's copy of the designed cover. It may still change a bit before final printing, but I thought you'd like to see it as near to completion as possible."

I was thinking of Henri this morning, praying in his memory, and then I was surprised to pull out the cover of this book from the Airborne Express envelope.

See how Henri is tilting his head, looking at us with his characteristic smile? See how Henri looked back then when he was writing and praying and living and sharing and growing? Here on the second anniversary of his death, Henri's picture appears smiling from the inside of an envelope.

What is Henri Nouwen to us today? Richard Jefferies in his book *The Story of My Heart* wrote, "It is eternity now. I am in the midst of it. It is about me in the sunshine; I am in it, as the butterfly in the light-laden air. Nothing has to come; it is now. Now is eternity; now is the immortal life."

What is Henri to us now? Surely living the immortal life. What was Henri to us back then? As you will see in the following reflections on Henri's life, he was a man of faith, a simple faith that did not get lost in academic, cumbersome definitions. Henri refused to allow his Christian faith to be categorized as Catholic or Evangelical. I think of Henri's expression of faith as I think of Walt Whitman's expression of the soul or Carl Sandburg's definition of a nation: all one soul, the people, yes, all one person.

During his life, Henri expressed the urgency for people to love one another, and he labored to remind us again and again that God made a promise to all of us: He will save us. "Hold faithfulness and sincerity as first principles," Confucius wrote. Hold faithfulness, Henri wrote in his books, said in his lectures, expressed in his letters. Be faithful to God, and do not be afraid. Yes, there is ugliness, but do not be afraid.

Last weekend I saw evidence of great destruction: mangled bodies, ruined marriages, a mother who could not complete her sentence when she tried to tell me about the death of her son on a basketball court. Paul the apostle wrote to the Corinthians, "We walk by faith, not by sight." The chaos and destruction I *saw* last weekend deeply disturbed me. And yet the order and birth of faith I see dripping down from the tip of a rhododendron leaf out my window defines eternity: water seeping into the earth after the rain, water of hope, water of the harvest.

Henri reminded us, during his lifetime, that, as Paul said, "Now is the accepted time."

A play on words, *Nouwen Then:* Henri as we see him now, a messenger of hope and salvation. Henri then: a messenger of hope and salvation. The difference being, in his death, in his absence, we are asked, again, to believe in God on our own, to love one another in the context of our individual souls. Paul said, "Let us not be weary in well doing." For many people, Henri was able to articulate the "well doing" that we seek during the confusing and difficult times that we sometimes have to endure. For others, Henri was able to corroborate what was already in their souls: that conviction that such "well doing" was already there, even in sadness.

And what is the purpose of well-doing? To be with God, someday, to be with the Father someday, to be in the light-laden air of eternity. It is true, it is all true.

Yes, there is divorce. Yes, there is death and disintegrating bodies. Yes, there are people who sustain great physical and mental damage. Yes, there is great sadness and pain in our lives, but there is also the rain and the seed, and there is the heat of God upon our cheeks.

Henri Nouwen zealously affected many people's definition of faith. May these personal reflections on Henri zealously affect you to look at the man on the cover of this book and smile back in agreement: God made us a promise. Beyond our suffering, God made us a promise that all will be well, and we must continue in our well-doing.

One

The Journey Toward Bethlehem

by
Christopher de Vinck

Dear Chris:
. . . Jean Vanier just left after a three-day visit in which he and a small accompaniment team reviewed my first five years in Daybreak. It was a very affirming visit, and I have made the decision to continue my life and work here and to deepen my vocation in the years to come by continuing to live in L'Arche. . . .

Henri Nouwen, December 19, 1991

Christopher de Vinck

Christopher de Vinck earned his doctorate in education from Columbia University, and he is presently the Supervisor of Humanities at Clifton High School in Clifton, New Jersey. He has spent the past twenty-two years as a high school English teacher and administrator.

In addition to his career in education, he has written eight books: *The Power of the Powerless* (Zondervan), *Only the Heart Knows How to Find Them* (Viking), *Augusta and Trab* (Macmillan), *Simple Wonders* (Zondervan), *Threads of Paradise* (Zondervan), *Songs of Innocence and Experience* (Viking), *The Book of Moonlight* (Zondervan), and *Love's Harvest* (Crossroad). He received two Christopher Awards for his books, invitations to speak throughout the country and at the Vatican, and has been published in the *New York Times*, the *Wall Street Journal*, the *Reader's Digest*, the *College Board Review*, *Guideposts*, *Good Housekeeping*, the *American Scholar*, the *Catholic Digest*, and *America*.

Dr. de Vinck and his wife, Roe, have been married for twenty-two years and live in Pompton Plains, New Jersey, with their three children: Karen, Michael, and David.

IN the spring of 1984, I was standing in line waiting for my coat following an awards ceremony in New York City. The Christophers, a nondenominational, interfaith movement started by Father James Keller, and based on the now famous theme, "It is better to light one candle than to curse the darkness," gives out annual awards to authors, organizations, and television producers who make a significant difference in the world. I was working for the Christophers at the time and found myself standing in line behind Henri Nouwen.

I had no idea who Henri Nouwen was, except that he wrote books and won a Christopher Award, and that he had an article in the Jesuit magazine *America* at the same time one of my poems appeared there. The first time I saw Henri's name was in that magazine. I thought it an odd name, and I was a bit annoyed that my poem had to share space on the page with someone else.

As the line slowly moved toward the coat-check room, Henri turned to me and said, "Hello. I am Henri Nouwen."

I answered, "We met before," and then I extended my hand. "On the pages of *America* magazine. I had a poem on the last page of an article you wrote."

Henri looked at me and said, right away, that he didn't know much about poetry, that he loved Gerard Manley Hopkins, and would I tell him something about poetry. We spoke briefly about William Carlos Williams, or, rather, I spoke briefly about Williams. Henri didn't know who the New Jersey poet was, but he was immediately interested and asked that I write to him.

"Where are you living?"

Henri wrote down his address on the award's program and handed my book to me. We were given our coats, and then we were both quickly swept up in the crowd as Henri disappeared. In my hand was an address:

Henri Nouwen
The Divinity School
Harvard University
Cambridge, Massachusetts 02138

I guess this guy works at Harvard, I said to myself. I folded the program in half and slipped it into my suit jacket, and then I drove home.

I did not know at the time that Henri and I were going to be friends. I did not know that we were to discover we were on the same journey. I did not realize who Henri was, did not realize that in his life he would touch many, many people with his honesty, his wisdom, his pain and joy. I did not realize that Henri was the spiritual leader for millions of men and women throughout the world. I thought he was a bright man with a Dutch accent who liked the poetry of Hopkins.

Dear Christopher:

Many thanks for your wonderful letter. It was really great to hear from you. I have often wondered how you were doing and how things were going with you and your family. Receiving your letter with all the good news about the expectation of your third child, the good news about your writing and poetry and about the possibility of a book with children's stories—all of that was a great joy to me.

By separate mail I have sent you books about my mother. Meanwhile, my life is going very well. I am going to Guatemala for ten days and from there I will go to France to live with Jean Vanier until January. Then I will be back at Harvard Divinity School. I have moved into a small house. I really hope that one day you can come to Cambridge for a visit.

While I am in France with Jean Vanier, I hope to try my hand with a few children's stories. I hope that it will be a good experience for me. If you write to me, I will continue to have my address at Harvard while I am in France. Any mail will be forwarded to me in France.

Thanks for staying in touch. May the Lord bless you and give you on-going joy in life.

Yours,

Henri

How was I to know who Henri Nouwen was? He thought my letter to him was wonderful, and he was excited to hear about the coming birth of my wife's and my third child. Henri was interested in writing children's books, and he was going to France, and he was moving into a little house in Cambridge, and he wanted me to come visit him. This is all that I knew about Henri Nouwen.

Still, from the first moment I met Henri, I felt as if I was his best friend. I came to find out quickly that this is how many people felt who knew Henri, through correspondence or through his writing.

He extended his warmth. He extended his interest. He extended an invitation to Harvard. He spoke with glee about Roe and my children. Henri made many people he met feel as if they were special, as if they mattered, as if they were someone extraordinary.

I have spent much of my life as a giver. I believed when I was a little boy that the saying "I AM THIRD" was written for me. God first, others second, and then myself, third. This notion that I am third influenced my life as a teacher, as a young man dating, as a husband, as a father, as a school administrator, and as a writer. I believed it was my vocation to love others, to serve others, to place my needs behind everyone else's. I believed it was my vocation to write in order to make a difference in peoples' lives. I struggled with my own ego, of course. I wanted to be the best writer, the best teacher, the best husband, the best father, and, in a way, I wanted to be better than most people. During my early struggles I think that I placed my life far down as the hero in the face of all that I did not know or understand.

In reality, I was a frightened boy, a lonely adolescent, a confused young adult. I stumbled into a teaching career because I knew that I liked books and people. I fell into a writing habit because a woman I loved did not fall in love with me, and I didn't know about drugs and liquor and sex so, well, I began to write. What is a man to do when he is in college and he wants to make love to a woman who doesn't love him? Find another woman? Find a needle? Find a drink? Find God? I found the work of William Carlos Williams and began to write my own poetry. And then I met Henri, and he seemed to like me for me. He didn't want anything. He didn't want an autograph, he didn't want me to give a speech. He just wanted to be friends. That puzzled me, because I did not have friends.

I spent my time being with Roe, raising our children, teaching, and writing—so much so that I had no time for anything else. Friendship takes time. Friendship demands attention. Friendship expects vulnerability. I didn't have time for friends, I didn't know that I needed attention, and I was not vulnerable to anyone except to my wife. I didn't realize how lonely I really was, even in our home with Roe and the children, even in the classroom with all my students around me, even in the quiet room where I write. I felt a loss, something missing, a part of me that was not whole. Of course I have come to understand that everyone feels this loneliness, but I didn't know what it was, and I didn't know who might understand. It seemed silly to tell Roe that I was lonely. How could that be? She loves me the way all men wished to be loved by a woman.

And then I learned who Henri Nouwen was. I found his books in the bookstores. I mentioned his name to my mother, and she said that she believed that Henri Nouwen is one of the holiest men she'd ever read. I heard that this Nouwen fellow knew congressman and cardinals, that he taught at Harvard and Yale and gave lectures throughout the world.

I thought I had discovered Henri Nouwen. (I didn't even pronounce his name correctly when I first saw him receive his Christopher Award in 1984.) I thought Henri Nouwen was a nice person who stole part of my page in America magazine. I didn't know, above all else, that Henri was a writer. I didn't know that he was, perhaps, a prophet. I didn't know that he maintained an active correspondence with at least five hundred people. I didn't know that he made people feel special and holy and loved and interesting. I didn't know that Henri invited many, many people into his home and into his heart. I didn't know that most people who met Henri believed they discovered him. I didn't know that Henri was on a journey. I didn't know that I was on the same journey. I didn't know that we are all, all on that same journey.

There are some people who are graced with a direct knowledge that we are on a path toward God. I think Walt Whitman knew. I think William Carlos Williams knew. So did my grandmother as she blessed me with a small cross on my forehead each night before I went to bed. My mother and father know of that journey. They carried my brother Oliver from his bed to the lawn for thirty-two years. They fed him for thirty-two years. They loved this boy, this blind, hopeless, blank child for thirty-two years, and they never cursed God for Oliver's affliction; they celebrated his life.

I didn't know Henri Nouwen was just like me in many ways. And I surely didn't know that Henri Nouwen was just like all of us in many ways. I didn't know that Henri whispered to us all, "Blow on the coal of your heart." I didn't know Henri was Job, that Henri was father, that Henri was friend, that Henri was neighbor, that Henri was the child, that Henri was the teacher, that Henri was the spiritual director.

As we make our way toward Bethlehem, as we make our way through our journey to the house of bread, what do we need? We need to know we have a soul. Yes. We need to know there is justice on this earth. Yes. We need to know there is an invisible self, an inside self. Yes. But we also need to know that there is a journey to be taken. We need to be nourished along the way. We need to know the direction, and we need to have fellow pilgrims. We cannot travel alone. We cannot face what Job faced alone. We stumble all the time, and when we do, we need others to help us up again. Even Christ stumbled under the weight of the cross as he made his way to salvation. And finally, in order for us to thrive, we need to have the courage to continue on our journey despite the obstacles, we need an open heart, we need faith, and we need to know when the journey ends and when it begins.

Two

Knowledge of the Journey

by
Philip Yancey

Dear Chris:
. . . After my wonderful time in France I made an
extremely revealing and eye-opening and moving trip to
Russia. On the one hand I experienced real oppression;
on the other hand, deep faith. This was my very first
experience of being in an Eastern European country and
it made me more aware than ever of the great privileges
that we enjoy as well as of the casualness with which we
accept the opportunity to speak freely about God and the
mysteries of God. The first and only question they asked
me at the customs in Moscow was "Do you have a Bible
with you?" and when I said "yes" they confiscated it
immediately. But when I went into the churches to wor-
ship (only a few were open in Russia) I experienced an
immense faith with an enormous tenacity and somehow
I sensed that Russians who have lived through the Tartar
oppression, through the Napoleonic Wars and through
the Nazi occupation, would also survive the Soviet

oppression and keep their faith alive in the midst of it all. Russians know what long-suffering is and have a patience that is centuries long. There is much to share with you about it, but I just want you to know that the journey was extremely important for my own spiritual life. . . .

Henri Nouwen, September 4, 1986

Philip Yancey

Philip Yancey is the author of the national bestsellers *The Jesus I Never Knew*, which was the ECPA Book of the Year in 1996, *What's So Amazing About Grace*, which was the ECPA Book of the Year in 1997. Yancey's other Gold Medallion award-winning books include *Where Is God When it Hurts*, *Disappointment with God*, and *The Gift Nobody Wants* (with Dr. Paul Brand). He has also written *In His Image* and *Fearfully and Wonderfully Made* (both with Dr. Paul Brand) and *Church: Why Bother?*

He is editor-at-large for *Christianity Today* magazine and co-editor of *The NIV Student Bible*. Yancey and his wife live in Colorado.

ONCE when I was dining with a group of writers, the conversation turned to letters we get from readers. Richard Foster and Eugene Peterson mentioned an intense young man who had sought spiritual direction from both of them. They had responded graciously, answering questions by mail and recommending books on spirituality. But Foster then learned that the same inquirer had also contacted Henri Nouwen. "You won't believe what Nouwen did," he said. "He invited this stranger to live with his community for a month so he could give him spiritual direction."

You would have to be a writer to appreciate fully Nouwen's action. We writers jealously protect our schedules and privacy. A few years ago I moved from downtown Chicago to rural Colorado specifically to put space between myself and the madding world outside. Yes, we may accept speaking engagements, answer letters, and even return phone calls from curious readers, but always we cultivate a private domain that no one else may enter. Henri Nouwen broke down such barriers of professionalism. His entire life, in fact, revealed a pattern of "holy inefficiency."

Trained in Holland as a psychologist and theologian, Nouwen spent his early years realizing his ambitions. He taught at Notre Dame, Yale, and Harvard, wrote more than a book a year on average, and traveled widely as a conference speaker. He had a résumé to die for—which was the problem, exactly. The pressing schedule and relentless competition were suffocating his own spiritual life.

Nouwen retreated to South America for six months, scouting a possible role for himself as a missionary in the Third World. The crushing needs in Bolivia and Peru, the language barrier, and a hectic speaking schedule on his return to the U.S. only made matters worse. Finally, Nouwen fell into the arms of L'Arche Community in France, a home for the seriously disabled. He felt so nourished by them that he agreed to become a priest in residence at a similar home in Toronto called Daybreak. There, Nouwen spent his last ten years, still writing and traveling to speak here and there but always returning to the haven of Daybreak.

It was from Nouwen that I first heard the phrase *downward mobility*. In a 1981 article in *Sojourners*, he wrote against the uncontrolled drive for prestige, power, and ambition—in short, the upward mobility—characteristic of American culture. "The great paradox which Scripture reveals to us is that real and total freedom can only be found through downward mobility. The Word of God came down to us and lived among us as a slave. The divine way is indeed the downward way."

Leaving a tenured position at an Ivy League school to settle among a community of the mentally challenged made no sense by any modern measure of success. When I first heard the news, I smiled at Nouwen's choice to live as a "fool for Christ." How wrong I was. He did not reach that decision as an act of self-sacrifice; he chose it for himself.

As he later reflected, "I liked to be at Yale, I liked to teach, but ... I felt I needed something else because my spiritual life was not deep. I am just a fragile person and I knew that I was not rooted deeply enough in Christ. There was not enough inner nurturedness in God. I wanted something more basic."

The invitation to join L'Arche came at a time when he felt on the edge of burnout, suffering from the incessant demands of upward mobility. He received a visit from the director of a L'Arche home, Jan Risse, on a mission from the group's founder. Jan visited Nouwen for a few days, cooked meals for him, and helped him in very practical ways. Nouwen kept expecting the inevitable request to give a lecture, write an article, offer a retreat. No such request came. L'Arche was bringing Nouwen grace pure and simple, no strings attached.

Jan's visit made such an impression that Nouwen asked his bishop for permission to join a L'Arche Community. For the first time in his life, he sensed God calling him to do something. He went to learn "what seminary and theology didn't teach me: how to love God and how to discover the presence of God in my own heart." In other words, he went there not to give up but to gain, not out of excess but out of need.

In Peru, Nouwen had been struck by the observation of a Maryknoll priest who said that missionary activity had changed from selling pearls to hunting for treasure. Living in the homes of the poor,

Nouwen learned that we minister to the needy not only to take Jesus to them but also to find Jesus within them.

While in Peru, Nouwen heard the news from Holland that his sister-in-law had given birth to a daughter with Down's syndrome. He wrote the family these words, not knowing that in a few years they would seem a prophetic insight into his decision to move to Daybreak:

> Laura is going to be important for all of us in the family. We have never had a "weak" person among us. We all are hardworking, ambitious, and successful people who seldom have had to experience powerlessness. Now Laura enters and shows us a totally new dependency. Laura, who always will be a child, will teach us the way of Christ as no one will ever be able to do.

I have two friends, Mike and Dee, who asked Nouwen for permission to visit him at Daybreak. Just as he had welcomed the young man seeking spiritual direction, he invited both my friends for a visit, along with their spouses. They have given me a glimpse of what Nouwen himself found at the L'Arche Community.

Mike and Dee arrived late in the evening and slept in one of the group homes. The next morning they met with Nouwen and other staff members, along with some of the mentally challenged, in a group meeting. Everyone sat in a circle. Some of the residents drooled, some rocked back and forth in their chairs, some slept. Mike led off, telling the group of how job pressures had led to a divorce and destroyed his family. He had remarried, but still he was caught up in a rat race of speaking engagements, writing assignments, management hassles, and travel, and he came to Daybreak because he knew that this was the very rat race Nouwen had escaped. He said he wanted to get away from it all, to withdraw from everyone he knew, to start over. But he didn't know how. His life was out of control.

During a break, one of the mentally-challenged residents came up to Mike. Standing inappropriately close to him, he jabbed him in the chest with his finger. "Too busy!" the man announced, proud of himself for having figured out Mike's dilemma.

"Yes, that's right," Mike replied. "That's exactly right. I'm just too busy."

"Too busy!" the man repeated, jabbing him again.

"You got it, pal. That's my problem."

Then the man asked a one-word question that Mike insists has haunted him ever since, "Why?" That's the question he had come to Daybreak to answer. Out of the mouth of babes came wisdom.

After the break, Dee spoke. Her first night had been very uncomfortable. She had arrived late in the evening, unprepared for what she would find in a home populated by the profoundly retarded. People strange in both behavior and appearance roamed the hallway outside her room, making inarticulate grunting noises, scratching the walls and doors. She checked the lock on the door several times and hardly slept.

Dee had traveled a long way for this meeting, however, and she forced herself to overcome inner resistance and share her struggles with this most intimidating group. As she spoke and began softly weeping, the young man next to her, a paraplegic in a wheelchair, reached over with a floppy motion and grabbed her hand. She had to fight the instinct to recoil. He stroked her hand gently and held it, and as she continued speaking his touch seemed to give her strength.

Afterward, Dee sought out the man in the wheelchair and thanked him for that gesture. Speaking with great effort, the sounds coming from deep in his throat, he said, "That's—what—hands—are—for."

"How little do we really know the power of physical touch," wrote Nouwen during his sojourn in Peru. He had just visited an orphanage where the children, starved for affection, fought for the privilege of touching him.

> These boys and girls only wanted one thing: to be touched, hugged, stroked, and caressed. Probably most adults have the same needs but no longer have the innocence and

unself-consciousness to express them. Sometimes I see humanity as a sea of people starving for affection, tenderness, care, love, acceptance, forgiveness, and gentleness. Everyone seems to cry: "Please love me." The cry becomes louder and the response so inaudible that people kill each other and themselves in despair. The little orphans tell more than we know. If we do not love one another, we kill one another. There is no middle road.

Henri Nouwen sat in the Hermitage Museum in St. Petersburg, Russia, for many hours meditating on Rembrandt's great painting, *The Return of the Prodigal Son*. While staring at the painting, Nouwen gained a new insight into the parable: the mystery that Jesus himself became something of a prodigal son for our sakes. "He left the house of his heavenly Father, came to a foreign country, gave away all that he had, and returned through a cross to his Father's home. All of this he did, not as a rebellious son but as the obedient son, sent out to bring home all the lost children of God . . . Jesus is the prodigal son of the prodigal father who gave away everything the Father had entrusted to him so that I could become like him and return with him to his father's home."

Among many lessons to be learned from the parable, two stood out for Nouwen: God's generosity, or *grace*, and the Son's way of expressing it, through the long journey of self-emptying, or *kenosis*.

God's love is shockingly personal. As Nouwen points out, "God rejoices. Not because the problems of the world have been solved, not because all human pain and suffering have come to an end, nor because thousands of people have been converted and are now praising him for his goodness. No, God rejoices because one of his children who was lost has been found."

In his book-length meditation on the Prodigal Son, Nouwen refers to another parable, Jesus' puzzling story of the laborers in the vineyard. For a long time, he confesses, a feeling of irritation welled up inside him when he read that parable, which has a landowner paying the same amount to those who worked one hour as to those who worked all day in the blazing heat. It had not occurred to him that the landowner might have wanted the workers of the early hours to rejoice in his generosity to the latecomers, grateful to see what a generous man he was. God, says Nouwen, looks at his people not as laborers earning their pay but as children of a family who are thrilled when those who have accomplished little are loved as much as those who accomplish a lot.

> God is so naive as to think that there would be great rejoicing when all those who spent time in his vineyard, whether a short time or a long term, were given the same attention. Indeed, he was so naive as to expect that they would all be happy to be in his presence that comparing themselves with each other wouldn't even occur to them. That is why he says with the bewilderment of a misunderstood lover: "Why should you be envious because I am so generous?" It is the same bewilderment that comes from the heart of the father who says to his jealous son: "My son, you are with me always, and all I have is yours." Here lies hidden the great call to conversion: to look not with the eyes of my own low-esteem, but with the eyes of God's love.

At Daybreak, Nouwen began truly to look with the eyes of God's love. Among those broken bodies and broken minds, his prestigious résumé meant nothing. All that mattered was whether he loved them. Unexpectedly, he had moved from leading to being led, he later reflected. Previously, he had believed that with age and maturity he would develop into a leader, more and more in control. Instead, when he entered the community of Daybreak, all such controls fell apart.

Nouwen once defined a community as "a place where the person you least want to live with always lives." If Bill did not like the priest's sermon, for example, he would interrupt Mass to tell him so. Nouwen found that his beautiful words and arguments often had no relevance to what the residents were experiencing. "When people have little intellectual capacity," he observed, "they let their hearts—their loving hearts, their angry hearts, their longing hearts—speak directly and often unadorned."

It took me a long time to feel safe in this unpredictable climate, and I still have moments in which I clamp down and tell everyone to shut up, get in line, listen to me, and believe in what I say. But I am also getting in touch with the mystery that leadership, for a large part, means to be led. I discover that I am learning many new things, not just about the pains and struggles of wounded people, but also about their unique gifts and graces. They teach me about joy and peace, love and care and prayer—what I could never have learned in any academy. They also teach me what nobody else could have taught me, about grief and violence, fear and indifference. Most of all, they give me a glimpse of God's first love, often at moments when I start feeling depressed and discouraged.

Nouwen became so attached to the people in his home, and so dependent on them, that he began taking them with him on his speaking trips. Whereas other well-known speakers might command an honorarium of $5000 or $10,000, Nouwen would ask for just $500 (which he would sign over to Daybreak) and a plane ticket for himself and a companion. A reporter for the *Wall Street Journal* remembers attending one such engagement in North Carolina. When Nouwen invited his friend Bill—the same one who interrupted Mass—to the microphone to speak, the reporter thought to himself that people had come a long way to hear Henri Nouwen, not Bill.

In order to give Bill support, Nouwen stood next to him on the stage. Bill looked out over the audience, and suddenly all his words failed him. He was overcome. He simply laid his head on Nouwen's shoulders and wept. Much that Nouwen said has passed from the memory of that North Carolina audience; the memory of Bill resting his head on a priest's shoulder has not. "I tell you the truth, anyone who will not receive the kingdom of God like a little child will never enter it," said Jesus. "And he took the children in his arms, put his hands on them and blessed them."

Daybreak assigned Nouwen one person to look after in particular: Adam (their relationship is celebrated in Nouwen's book, *Adam: God's Beloved*, published postmortem in 1997). Adam was the weakest person in the ten-person home. Although in his twenties, Adam could not speak, dress or undress himself, could not walk alone or eat without help. Instead of counseling Ivy League students and juggling a busy schedule, Nouwen had to learn a new set of skills: how to feed, change, and bathe Adam. He ministered not to intellectuals but to a young man who was considered by many a vegetable, a useless person who should not have been born. Yet Nouwen gradually learned that he, not Adam, was the chief beneficiary to this strange, mis-fitted relationship.

From the hours spent with Adam, Nouwen gained an inner peace so fulfilling that it made most of his other, more high-minded tasks seem boring and superficial by contrast. Early on, as he sat beside that silent, slow-breathing child-man, he realized how violent and marked with rivalry and competition, how obsessive, was his prior drive toward success in academia and Christian ministry. From Adam he learned that "what makes us human is not our mind but our heart, not our ability to think but our ability to love. Whoever speaks about Adam as a vegetable or animal-like creature misses the sacred mystery that Adam is fully capable of receiving and giving love." From Adam, Henri Nouwen learned—gradually, painfully, shamefully—that the way up is down.

This is what Henri learned from Adam:

> Keep your eyes on the one who refuses to turn stones into bread, jump from great heights or rule with great temporal power. Keep your eyes on the one who says, "Blessed are the poor, the gentle, those who mourn and those who hunger and thirst for the righteousness; blessed are the merciful, the peacemakers and those who are persecuted in the cause of the uprightness." . . . Keep your eyes on the one who is poor

with the poor, weak with the weak and rejected with the rejected. That one is the source of all peace.

Henry David Thoreau, unlike Nouwen, withdrew from society because of his failure to win recognition as a writer. When society proved unresponsive to his work, he sought the solace of solitude. Later, asked to explain, he said, "I went to the woods because I wished to live deliberately, to front only the essential facts of life, and see if I could not learn what it had to teach and not, when I came to die, discover that I had not lived."

Nouwen, who sought some seclusion from an all-too-responsive society, ended up learning the same lesson as Thoreau. The first and greatest commandment is to love God with all our heart, soul, and mind—but how can we do so in a world full of distraction and busyness? Daybreak gave Nouwen the time, and the right environment, to develop a way of seeing.

In fact, though others looking at Nouwen's career path see a pattern of downward mobility, Nouwen himself saw a form of "inward mobility." He withdrew in order to look inward, to learn how to love God and be loved by God. He described the search early on, in *The Genesee Diary*, citing a passage from Robert Pirsig's *Zen and the Art of Motorcycle Maintenance*. Pirsig describes two kinds of mountain climbers. Both place one foot in front of the other, breathe in and out at the same rate, stop when tired, and move forward when rested. But the "ego-climber" misses the whole experience. He does not notice the beautiful passage of sunlight through the trees. He looks up the trail to see what's ahead even though he just looked for the same thing a second ago. "His talk is forever about somewhere else, something else. He's here but he's not here. What he is looking for, what he wants, is all around him, but he doesn't want that because it *is* all around him."

Nouwen once lived his spiritual life like that. Books to read, skills to learn, talks to give, letters to answer—these things pressed in on him so that he could not see that God was all around him. Meanwhile he was trying to peer ahead, farther down the trail.

When he asked advice of Mother Teresa, she counseled, "Spend an hour a day in contemplative prayer and commit no conscious sins." Nouwen had difficulty carving out an hour a day, but he did manage a half-hour a day. He reports in *Life of the Beloved* that he began to conceive of prayer differently: not as a time to talk but to listen, a quiet, attentive time of "listening to the voice that says good things about me." For someone as insecure and driven with doubts as Nouwen, that was a hard discipline.

Nouwen practiced what the apostle Paul called "the renewing of your mind," and for him praying developed into a time of re-imagining. All day images from television, movies, and advertisements fill our minds, along with judgments, guilt-messages, temptations, to-do lists. Prayer offers a time to purge those messages and replace them with the mind of Christ. Nouwen once saw the movie *Stuntman* just before Advent. It overwhelmed him. "The movie was so filled with images of greed and lust, manipulation and exploitation, fearful and painful sensations, that it filled all the empty spaces that could have been blessed by the spirit of Advent," he said. Prayer helped to replace those images. And the mundane, even tedious tasks involved in caring for Adam gave him an extended daily time of silence in which the act of service could do its slow, healing work.

When he moved to Daybreak, Nouwen wondered about the negative effects of withdrawal. Would he suffer from living "out of the loop"? Instead, like Thomas Merton, he found a life of withdrawal need not lead to isolation. Peter France, who has written extensively on hermits, draws a parallel to scientists who work alone in search of cures for diseases. Most of Nouwen's followers found his work growing more relevant, not less, during his time at Daybreak.

A pastor friend of mine named Bill used to use the illustration of an old hand-operated pump. He sometimes felt like such a pump, he said. Everyone who came along would reach up and pump vigorously a few times, and each time he felt something drain out of him. Finally, he was approaching a point of burnout, when he had nothing more to give. He felt dry, desiccated. In the midst of this period, Bill went on a week-long retreat and expressed these thoughts to his designated spiritual director, a very wise woman. He expected her to offer soothing words about what a wonderful, sacrificial person he was. Instead, she said, "Bill, there's only one thing to do if your reservoir is dry. You've got to go deeper." He realized on that retreat that if his outward journey were to continue, he needed to give a higher priority to his inner journey.

For the same reason, Nouwen concluded that "the basis of all ministry rests not in the moral life, but in the mystical life."

> Nobody has to prove to me that prayer makes a difference. Without prayer I become irritable, tired, heavy of heart, and I lose the Spirit who directs my attention to the needs of others instead of my own. Without prayer, my attention moves to my own preoccupation. I become cranky and spiteful and often I experience resentment and a desire for revenge.

Like every other contemplative, Nouwen learned that mystical life involves a paradox: though it must be received as a gift, the gift comes only after serious effort. "We cannot plan, organize or manipulate God; but without a careful discipline, we cannot receive him either." Around us, the images of the world call for us to pamper, exercise, nourish, develop, and display our bodies. But how many give as much attention to developing the soul as to the body?

In *The Living Reminder*, a book for pastors, Henri Nouwen coined a remarkable and daring phrase: "the ministry of absence." Ministers do a disservice, he says, if they witness only to God's presence and do not prepare others to experience the times when God seems absent. "The minister is not called to cheer people up but modestly to remind them that in the midst of pains and tribulations the first sign of the new life can be found and a joy can be experienced which is hidden in the midst of sadness." Thus an authentic ministry requires the art of creative withdrawal.

The Road to Daybreak, chronicles Henri Nouwen's decision to move to Daybreak and put into practice his own form of creative withdrawal. In a review, Harold Fickett wrote that he found it disappointing to read that the same problems described a decade earlier in *The Genesee Diary*—writing projects, deficient friendships, unrequited love, hurt feelings at perceived slights—continued to plague Nouwen. Fickett explained, "It's disappointing in exactly the same way it's disappointing to be ourselves—the same person with the same problems who learns and then must relearn again and again the basic lessons of religious faith. Nouwen does not spare himself or us the embarrassment of this perennial truth."

Fickett has put his finger on a defining characteristic of Nouwen: indeed he does not spare himself, or his readers, the embarrassment of truth, even when that truth makes him look bad. *The Living Reminder* gives an explanation for his disarming style. The suffering most frequently encountered in ministry, Nouwen says, is "a suffering of memories": feelings of alienation, loneliness, separation, feelings of anxiety, fear, suspicion. Buried deep inside, these memories release a form of toxin that attacks the center of our being. Good memories we display in the form of trophies, diplomas, and scrapbooks; the other, painful memories remain hidden from view, where they escape healing and cause enduring harm.

Our spontaneous response to such wounding memories, Nouwen says, is to act as if they did not happen, to not talk about them and think instead about happier things. But by the deliberate act of not-remembering, we allow the suppressed memories to gain strength and exert a crippling power over our functioning as human beings. Nouwen had the courage to turn the spotlight on those deep places, to expose the wounding memories within himself. He gained a loyal following of readers in part because he took the risk of demonstrating that his own story, all of it, could display God's ongoing redemptive work. The only true healer he said, in a memorable phrase, is a "wounded healer."

Do not be misled: Nouwen did not share the modern penchant for "telling all" about sexual fantasies, childhood cruelties, and family insults. His fund of childhood depravities was rather small; from the age of five he had desires to be a priest, and he acted out the role with a toy altar, tabernacle, and vestments. Thus he never tasted many of the sins that grab the headlines today. The sins he exposed in himself as an adult were more hidden, and more intractable.

In *The Return of the Prodigal Son*, Nouwen found himself identifying most closely with the "virtuous" elder brother. As he wrote, "The lostness of the resentful 'saint' is so hard to reach precisely because it is so closely wedded to the desire to be good and virtuous."

> I know, from my own life, how diligently I have tried to be good, acceptable, likable, and a worthy example for others. There was always the conscious effort to avoid the pitfalls of sin and the constant fear of giving in to temptation. But with all of that there came a seriousness, a moralistic intensity— and even a touch of fanaticism—that made it increasingly difficult to feel at home in my Father's house. I became less free, less spontaneous, less playful....
>
> The more I reflect on the elder son in me, the more I realize how deeply rooted this form of lostness really is and how hard it is to return home from there. Returning home from a lustful escapade seems so much easier than returning home from a cold anger that has rooted in the deepest corners of my being.

I once heard Nouwen cite Jesus' instruction that his disciples should be "in the world but not of the world." He added a characteristic twist: "I have found it easier to be in the world and not of it than to be in the church and not of it." The priest or pastor is constantly tempted to see himself as the answer-giver, the spiritual director, the dispenser of grace and not its recipient. To fight that temptation, Nouwen circled back again and again to his failures and inadequacies.

He spoke often of his restlessness and loneliness, of the pervading sense of "living as though I do not yet have a home." Risking gossip, he wrote of emotional attachments to friends that only his priestly vows kept him from consummating. The "wound of loneliness" was to him like the Grand Canyon, he said: "... a deep incision in the surface of existence that has become an inexhaustible source of beauty and self-understanding." That insight typifies Nouwen's approach to ministry. He did not promise a way out of loneliness, for himself or for anyone else. Rather, he held out the promise of redemption through it.

In *Making All Things New* he wrote what could stand as an epitaph for his journey:

> What matters is to listen attentively to the Spirit and to go obediently where we are being led, whether to a joyful or a painful place. Poverty, pain, struggle, anguish, agony, and even inner darkness may continue to be part of our experience. They may even be God's way of purifying us. But life is no longer boring, resentful, depressing, or lonely because we have come to know that everything that happens is part of our way to the house of the Father.

I met Henri Nouwen in person only once, on a visit to Daybreak. First, we visited in his office, swapping publisher stories and comparing some of the topics we each planned to write on. Somewhat embarrassed, I mentioned that I was finishing up a book titled *Disappointment With God*. Instead of frowning at the title, he grew positively excited, gesticulating nonstop with his hands and telling me of his own experiences of disappointment. At one point he jumped to his feet, rushed over to the wall, and removed a print of a Van Gogh painting. "Here, this is what I mean," he said. "This captures the mood. It's yours. Take it as my gift."

When lunch time came, I tucked my newly acquired artwork under my arm and followed him on a wooden walkway that led across construction mud to the room where he lived. It had a single bed, one bookshelf, and a few pieces of Shaker-style furniture. The walls were unadorned except for a print of another Van Gogh painting— Nouwen once contributed to a book called *Van Gogh and God*—and a few religious symbols. A Daybreak staff person brought in a bowl of Caesar salad, a flask of wine, and a loaf of bread. No fax machine, no computer, no calendar posted on the wall—in this room, at least,

Nouwen had found serenity. The church "industry" seemed very far away.

Thoreau wrote that "Most of the luxuries, and many of the so-called comforts of life, are not only not indispensable, but positive hindrances to the elevation of mankind. With respect to the luxuries and comforts, the wisest have ever lived a more simple and meager life than the poor.... None can be an impartial or wise observer of human life but from the vantage ground of what we should call voluntary poverty." Glancing around, then mentally comparing Nouwen's surrounding to my own office full of machines, books, and *things*, I felt a twinge of envy. Yes, he had secretaries to handle correspondence and a religious sister to prepare his meals. Yes, a vow of poverty eliminated worries about IRS payments and royalty statements, and a vow of obedience simplified his process of decision-making. But wasn't that the point? He had shed these encumbrances out of commitment to something higher.

And what was that something higher? All morning Nouwen had been talking about his friend Adam. "You are here on a very special occasion!" he told me. "Today is Adam's birthday! He turns twenty-six, and his parents and brothers will be here for a very special celebration of the Eucharist."

Already that day, Nouwen told me, he had spent nearly two hours preparing Adam. I had read Nouwen's own description of this daily process:

> It takes me about an hour and a half to wake Adam up, give him his medication, carry him into his bath, wash him, shave him, clean his teeth, dress him, walk him to the kitchen, give him his breakfast, put him in his wheelchair and bring him to the place where he spends most of the day with therapeutic exercises....
>
> He does not cry or laugh. Only occasionally does he make eye contact. His back is distorted. His arm and leg movements are twisted. He suffers from severe epilepsy and, despite heavy medication, sees few days without grand mal seizures. Sometimes, as he grows suddenly rigid, he utters a

howling groan. On a few occasions I've seen one big tear roll down his cheek.

After lunch we adjourned to a small chapel for the service. With solemnity, but also a twinkle in his eye, Nouwen led the liturgy in honor of Adam's birthday. Adam, unable to talk and profoundly disabled, gave no sign of comprehension, although he did appear to recognize that his family had come. He drooled throughout the ceremony and grunted loudly a few times.

I must admit I had a fleeting doubt as to whether this was the best use of the busy priest's time. I have heard Henri Nouwen speak and have read many of his books. He has much to offer. Could not someone else take over the manual chores? Back in his office, when I cautiously broached the subject with Nouwen himself, he informed me that I had completely misinterpreted him. "I am not giving up anything," he insisted. "It is I, not Adam, who gets the main benefit from our friendship."

The rest of the afternoon Nouwen kept circling back to my question, as if he could not believe I could ask such a thing. He kept bringing up various ways he had benefited from his relationship with Adam. Truly, he was enjoying a new kind of spiritual peace, acquired not within the stately quadrangles of Yale or Harvard, but by the bedside of incontinent Adam. I left Daybreak convicted of my own spiritual poverty, I who so carefully arrange my writer's life to make it efficient and single-focused.

It had been difficult for him at first, Nouwen admitted. Physical touch, affection, and the messiness of caring for an uncoordinated person did not come easily. But he had learned to love Adam, truly to love him. In the process he had learned what it must be like for God to love us—spiritually uncoordinated, disabled, capable of responding only with what must seem to God like inarticulate grunts and groans. Indeed, working with Adam had taught him the humility and emptiness achieved by desert monks only after much discipline. The time he spent caring for Adam had become an indispensable time of meditation.

Henri Nouwen has said that all his life two voices competed inside him. One encouraged him to succeed and achieve, while the other called him simply to rest in the comfort that he was *the beloved* of God. Only in the last decade of his life did he truly listen to that second voice.

Ultimately Nouwen concluded that "the goal of education and formation for the ministry is continually to recognize the Lord's voice, his face, and his touch in every person we meet." Reading that description in his book *Gracias!*, I understand why he did not think it a waste of time to invite a seeking stranger to live with him for a month or to devote hours each day to the menial care of Adam.

As I recently thumbed through the books on my Nouwen shelf, I came across three books that he had inscribed to me after my visit. "Thank you for giving me the courage to keep writing!" he had written in one. I had left Daybreak feeling convicted and ashamed, an intrusive journalist wasting a busy man's time. Nouwen, though, had harbored a very different memory, of a fellow-seeker, one beloved of God. Even now, after his death, he gives that gift to me afresh.

I miss Henri Nouwen. For some, his legacy consists of his many books, for others his role as a bridge between Catholics and Protestants, for others his distinguished career at Ivy League universities. For me, though, a single image captures him best: the energetic priest, hair in disarray, using his restless hands as if to fashion a homily out of thin air, celebrating an eloquent birthday Eucharist for an unresponsive child-man so damaged that many parents would have had him aborted. A better symbol of the Incarnation, I can hardly imagine.

Three

Nourishment for the Journey

by

Luci Shaw

Dear Chris:
. . . God truly cares for those who follow his loving guid-
ance. He has made that promise to you and to your fam-
ily and he will not disappoint you. The only thing God
asks of you is full, unwavering faith and trust. . . .
                              Henri Nouwen, March 3, 1988

Luci Shaw

Luci Shaw was born in 1928 in London, England, and has lived in Canada, Australia, and the U.S. A 1953 graduate of Wheaton College, she became co-founder and later president of Harold Shaw Publishers. Since 1988 she has been Writer in Residence at Regent College, Vancouver.

Shaw is well known as a retreat facilitator in church settings and lectures in North America and abroad on topics such as art and spirituality, the poetic imagination, and journal-writing as an aid to spiritual and artistic growth. She is a charter member and vice president of the Chrysostom Society of Writers, and author of seven volumes of poetry, including *Polishing the Petoskey Stone* (Shaw, 1990) and *Writing the River* (Regent Publishing, 1997). She has edited three poetry anthologies and a festschrift, *The Swiftly Tilting Worlds of Madeleine L'Engle*, and her work has been widely anthologized. She has also authored several non-fiction prose books, the most recent being *Water My Soul: Cultivating the Interior Life* (Zondervan, 1998). She has also co-authored three books with Madeleine L'Engle, *Winter Song* (Shaw), *Friends for the Journey* (VineBooks), and *A Prayer Book for Spiritual Friends* (Augsburg). She has five grown children, and she and her husband, John Hoyte, live in Bellingham, Washington.

M Y senses are the five wide-open windows of my soul. Does this sounds too "poetic," too embarrassingly sentimental to be real? It is, nevertheless, a rational observation that my imagination verifies. My senses—sight, smell, touch, hearing, taste—welcome the arrows of morning sunlight (and with that light comes insight, in-*sight!*) into the room of rather drab, functional furniture which is my logical mind. The connections flow naturally. When I see the green ferns and Oregon grape and feel the velvet moss in the verdant ravine under my study window, I think *growing*. When I breathe into my lungs the spiced sharpness of morning mist drifting over our Pacific Northwest lake, I think *the air of prayer*. When I look up at looming, capped-with-snow Mt. Baker, with its wisp of vapor, I think *God-strength, God-presence*. The thunder of breakers on the pebbled shore sounds in my ears like the voice of God. The surging tides of Puget Sound suggest to me the push and pull of my own journey, torn between faith and questioning.

You see, I have always been a natural skeptic, an investigator of the status quo, a sharp-eyed observer for whom the reality beneath the surface of things is of prime importance.

Brought up in a family with a tight system of Christian belief, I desperately *wanted* to cling, like a rider on a runaway horse, to what my parents told me was true. But my logical mind always asked, "What about all those who *don't* subscribe to orthodox Christianity? Who search out their own paths to God? Are they all fatally mistaken? And if God is a spirit, invisible, how can I know him? I believe Jesus came in the flesh to show us who God was, but how am I supposed to experience the reality of a God-man who lived and died two thousand years ago? Even with the tutelage of the Holy Spirit, can I be certain that what I experience of spiritual reality is not fantasy, or spiritual wish-fulfillment? How can I know and believe anything, for sure?"

I wanted to *know*, with a degree of certainty, that what I said with my lips, in my poems, as a public speaker, was true at the deepest levels in my heart. My active imagination, which sometimes widens into real faith, is coupled with a tendency to distrust things that don't seem susceptible to rational proof. When I'm with a very conservative group I find myself playing devil's advocate, presenting an alternative view, exploring other options just to balance things out. With more "liberal" thinkers, I'm the advocate for orthodoxy.

Where one part of me is eager to pin faith down, like a bug on a board, where I can see it, examine and control it, another part of me is restless, shaking at the reins, wanting to explore all the other possibilities, knowing that even if I achieved it, watertight certainty is like legalism: it jettisons mystery, renders faith unnecessary, grabs the control from God's hands, and sets up a grid of human rules instead, which gives us a false sense of safety. Faith is more like charting a course through Puget Sound, among all the islands and hidden reefs. We can see the islands and steer our boat clear of obvious obstacles, but the underwater rocks and sandbars are mysteries we cannot fathom, places where we must trust the charts and the skipper's experience.

These conflicting seismic rumblings shook my Christian certainties over the years. But my internal spiritual incongruities finally erupted, with the force of a volcano, when out of the blue, Harold, my husband of thirty-three years, father of my five children, a man of God who had never smoked, was diagnosed with lung cancer. During the sixteen traumatic months between the diagnosis and his death, I began to keep a daily, reflective journal. Those journal entries appear in *God in the Dark*, a painful book to write, in which I grappled with the problem of suffering, with the reality of God's presence and love, with the devastation of seeing my heart-companion diminishing in body, drawing further into himself, being cut off from me. And as he was wasting away, I was caught again between believing for his healing and facing my own profound fears and doubts that God was real and that he would be there for us.

How did Henri Nouwen enter the picture? I was given a copy of *The Genesee Diary*, the journal he kept during his seven months of seclusion in a Trappist monastery. There he attempted to come to grips with his own deepest questions, to strip away the glittering image that had been projected by his role as a gifted and popular writer and speaker, to draw closer to God. I felt immense comfort as I learned that some of my questions had been his questions too. His very personal published journal, like my own, never written for publication, allowed me the privilege of glimpsing his unguarded soul and learning with him as he learned from God and his brother monks.

For instance, his comments about Thomas, the rationalist, the disciple of doubt, reached me forcefully: "Didymus, the name of Thomas, means 'twin,' as the Gospel says, and … all of us are 'two people,' a doubting one and a believing one." Though Thomas doubted the reality of Jesus' resurrection, "he kept faithful to the community of the apostles. In that community the Lord appeared to him and strengthened his faith." During Harold's illness and my bereavement, I found this to be a fruitful pattern for my own dilemma. In spite of my hard questions, my Episcopal church family became for me, week by week, the context in which I was able "to recognize the Lord again."

It's still true. The body of the church reinforces its individual parts when they are weak, including me, just as when I have a toothache on the right side of my mouth I am prompted to let the left side take over the chewing for a while. Often I have felt this strength of being "carried along" like a small boat in a flowing current, by the community of faith. Every week in the Eucharist I participate in the old exchange: At Communion I bring to the altar all my flaws and failings, handing over my fears and skepticism and inadequacy, and Christ gives me himself instead, feeding me body and blood, his food for the soul, which strengthens me for the journey of the coming week.

Over the years, whenever I have re-read *The Genesee Diary*, I have found wisdom and a way of penetrating to the heart of my own needs. Like many of the students who have taken my journal-writing workshops, I find Nouwen's *Diary* a wonderful model for entering the process of contemplative reflection through a journal. And to students hesitant to start a journal because they are intimidated by the blank pages, or who think they have nothing profound or valid or interesting to say, I quote these words, excerpted from Nouwen's *Reflections on Theological Education*:

> Most students … think that writing means writing down ideas, insights, visions. They feel that they must first have something to say before they can put it down on paper. For

them writing is little more than recording a pre-existent thought.

But with this approach true writing is impossible. *Writing is a process in which we discover what lives in us. The writing itself reveals what is alive* ... [italics mine]. The deepest satisfaction of writing is precisely that it opens up new spaces within us of which we were not aware before we started to write. To write is to embark on a journey whose final destination we do not know. Thus, creative writing requires a real act of trust. We have to say to ourselves, "I do not yet know what I carry in my heart, but I trust that it will emerge as I write." Writing is like giving away the few loaves and fishes one has, trusting that they will multiply in the giving. Once we dare to "give away" on paper the few thoughts that come to us, we start discovering how much is hidden underneath ... and gradually come in touch with our own riches.

Such words free us, nudging us into the kind of confidence in the process that eases our way into writing as a way of discovering and articulating who we are before God. They urge us to trust God and our own hearts, and trusting results in fresh and surprising insights that bring great personal enrichment for ourselves and, through us, to those whom our lives touch. Often after reading one of his books, Nouwen's silver words seem to hang in the air over my days, reassuring, refreshing as a shower in drought time. Blessing me, or challenging me.

Let me describe some of the life circumstances in which Henri Nouwen and I intersected as my thoughts and prayers followed his. Like Henri, I struggled for most of my life with my own yearnings for approval, affirmation, recognition. Paradoxically, those yearnings grew like an addiction to a drug the more approval, affirmation, recognition I received. Like him, I realized that the only resolution to such deep needs was to let Jesus himself fill that lonely, hungry place inside me, to feel his approval, to rest in that alone. And that I needed to lift my heart away from myself, to set my love free to rise singly and purely to God. Like Henri, I wanted intimacy with God, but my very active life, full of diverse and compelling interests, often robbed me of the quiet, meditative time that is the prerequisite for such intimacy. This is a dilemma that has not yet found its resolution in my life—and may not while I am mortal. But I have come to believe that as long as the desire is there, as long as I don't become apathetic and complacent, that I am being drawn, as by a magnet, toward the Being in whom my ultimate longings will be satisfied. Now that Henri is in heaven, I am deeply happy that he has found what he was searching for and that I may some day join him.

Another thing. I used to "catastrophize" difficulties out of all proportion, to allow relatively minor rebuffs or perceived rejections to send me spiraling down into depression. I have often felt like a loaded, cocked pistol ready for some emotion, some small finger of negative feeling to pull the trigger. Nouwen, quoting his Genesee abbot John Eudes, in his own, similar predicament, comments that it is "not that your feelings are totally illegitimate. In fact, you might have a good reason to feel rejected. But the problem is that your response has no proportion to the nature of the event." Instead, he counsels, we should learn to *nuance* our responses, to learn to see ourselves and our situation more truly, through God's eyes, and find a more authentic perspective. I remind myself of this often, and it has helped me immeasurably.

An impatient, often restless person, I've had to learn a great deal about slowing down and waiting, often frustrating processes that seem like a waste of time. The Psalms are full of waiting: "We wait in hope for the LORD; he is our help and our shield" (33:20); "I will always wait in patience; I will praise you more and more" (71:14); "Be strong and take heart and wait for the LORD" (27:14); "I lay my requests before you and wait in expectation"(5:3); "My soul waits for the Lord more than watchmen wait for the morning, more than watchmen wait for the morning" (130:6). (In that repeated phrase we feel the watchers' eager anticipation for daybreak after what seems like an endless night.) Waiting seems to be an inevitable part of the human condition, especially frustrating in this age in which we demand instant gratification.

I only began to come to terms with waiting, and to learn its enormous value, after listening to a Nouwen tape on "The Spirituality of Waiting." And I like to couple Nouwen's words, "Waiting is a period of learning. The longer we wait, the more we hear about him for whom we are waiting," with Eugene Peterson's paraphrase of Romans 8:22–25: "Waiting does not diminish us, any more than waiting diminishes a pregnant mother. We are *enlarged in the waiting*" (italics added). I have begun to understand that during the times of waiting God is as vibrantly at work within us as new life and growth is at work within an expectant mother. If, through the Spirit of God, we have been united with the Father in dynamic relationship, if God has sown his Gospel seed in us, then Jesus is being formed within us, you and me, little by little, day by day, just as a human embryo grows to become a fetus and develops incrementally into a human baby. But we all need to *wait* if the Word is to become flesh in us and our potential is to mature into the reality for which we were created.

In this context of procreation and birth, Nouwen gave me a vital metaphor for understanding and dealing with my finite knowledge of God, a human limitation that had, in part, led to my existential questions about divine reality. During an address at an arts conference, he gave an illustration that printed itself vividly in my imagination. He told of twins, waiting, seed-like, in their mother's belly, warm, protected, blind, in the dark, unknowing about what lies ahead for them. As I listened to these introductory words my heart gave a quiver; I had a feeling about where his narrative was leading and that it might present me with a new understanding of my present human darkness and my ultimate place in God. The twins tell each other how much they feel at home in their fetal state, contented in their secure comfort in the womb, floating in amniotic fluid, yet safely tethered by their umbilical cords. But as their faculties and bodies develop they begin to wonder, to ask questions about their future. Finally, one of them says to the other, "Have you heard? Someday soon we'll be pushed out into the light, and there'll be this ... this thing called a *mother*. We'll see her face!"

Nouwen's story gave me the needed analogy. Now, in this life, we are like seeds all in the place of unknowing in the womb of God, growing towards our ultimate release into the light of God's presence, where we'll "know as we are known."

Recently I bought a copy of Nouwen's *In the Name of Jesus*. Much of the substance of that little book (Nouwen does so much in the narrow space of his short paperbacks!) deals with Henri's own lessons in giving away what power God gave him, sharing it with those who are powerless, in this book the severely disturbed or physically disabled people of L'Arche Community in Ontario, Canada. This directive, to give our power away, goes directly against our twentieth-century cultural grain. There is much discussion about how the disenfranchised are to achieve "empowerment." This process often seems to boil down to the seizing of power for themselves by people, or cultures, or nations, frequently by violent and destructive means.

Power has always been obsessive, whether in international political feuds or in personal relationships, but the idea of "empowerment" has become a cultural catchword in this generation. This may be because in the past there have been such outrageous abuses of power, of dictators over their populaces, of church leaders over members of their congregations, of parents over their children, of husbands over their wives. Perhaps some redress was deemed necessary. When we feel powerless, the thing we desire most fiercely is to gain (or regain) a sense of control and autonomy over our own lives.

We can talk endlessly about power for good versus power for evil, but it has long been understood that no matter what its motivation, personal power may corrupt, and the struggle for power for its own sake nearly always creates conflict that results in the destruction or annihilation of another.

Is this the result that God had in mind when he spoke our radiant world into being? The magnificent, continuing act of Creation shows an astonishing kind of power for beauty and for good. And when, in the supreme Creative Act, God sent the Son into our world, en-fleshed, and provided for the ongoing presence of Jesus in the Holy Spirit, there was never a hint manifested of destructive or selfish power. The gift of God's power was bestowed on us to help us change in ways that all our own effort and energy could never achieve, to move us out of the kingdom of darkness into the realm of light. As the apostle Peter put it in Acts 10: "God anointed Jesus . . . with the Holy Spirit and power. . . . He went around doing good and healing all who were under the power the devil" (v. 38), which describes the classic confrontation of destructive, evil power with the power of good to heal and make whole.

We hear a lot these days about "upward mobility"—that desire for elevated status, greater wealth, more influence, increased control. And the social scientists today have cajoled us into a new idolatry—the worship of self, of our *selves*. Now, I know that it's important for us to grow a healthy self-image. I absolutely acknowledge that we should be able to regard ourselves with respect for our integrity, our personal growth. We need to live out the image of God in us by loving ourselves as God has loved us, unconditionally. But I believe that our self-absorption and self-ism, like so many other corrective measures, have been taken to an extreme. With self-ism as the new idolatry, with becoming empowered as the new objective in life, with material values having risen to the top rung of the ladder of success, with anything that we cannot see, touch, prove, and *use* being discounted as irrelevant, spiritual and moral values have been dismissed or marginalized in this age of upward mobility.

How refreshing it is, in this context, to think of the *downward mobility* of Jesus, who left behind the magnificence and richness of heaven, who stripped himself of his sovereign splendor, who was willing to undergo poverty and abuse and rejection, to be out of step with his age. Listen to the prophetic words of Isaiah: "He will not shout or cry out or raise his voice in the streets. A bruised reed he will not break, and a smoldering wick he will not snuff out" (42:2–3). No arrogant power demonstrated there! Jesus most often works quietly, healing gently, restoring us even when we feel most weak and useless.

In Philippians 2 we hear an astonishing description of how Jesus relinquished power. Listen to these radical words of the apostle Paul, as Eugene Peterson renders them in *The Message*: "Do me a favor:

Agree with each other, love each other, be deep-spirited friends. Don't push your way to the front; don't sweet-talk your way to the top. Put yourself aside, and help others get ahead. Don't be obsessed with getting your own advantage. Forget yourselves.... Think of yourselves the way Christ Jesus thought of himself. He had equal status with God but didn't think so much of himself that he had to cling to the advantages of that status no matter what. Not at all. When the time came, he set aside the privileges of deity and took on the status of a slave, became *human!*" The NRSV concludes the passage like this: "He emptied himself ... and became obedient to the point of death—even death on a cross."

Jesus allowed himself to be categorized as a criminal, relinquishing any reputation for respectability. In the Greek, to "empty oneself" has the sense, in this passage, of a waterfall *continually pouring itself* over a cliff edge. This is the kind of Jesus love that Henri Nouwen exemplified so truly, so consistently. He knew the ultimate power of continually sharing his power with the powerless.

My one face-to-face encounter with Henri Nouwen vividly illustrates this last conviction—that God gives us power so that we may give it away to others. I was appointed as the "point person" to coordinate a conference on religion and the arts in Berkeley, California, with many prominent writers, artists, and lecturers scheduled to participate. But six weeks before the scheduled conference date all our attempts to find a leader for the culminating worship service had failed. In a phone discussion, the name of Henri Nouwen came up. "But he's in such demand, I'm sure he's already booked solid," I demurred. Greg Wolfe, the editor of the journal *Image*, which was sponsoring the event, responded, "It's a long shot, but let's invite him anyway. He can always say 'no.'" Copies of the magazine and an outline of events were forwarded to Nouwen in Canada and almost immediately on receiving them he called us: "It's just the kind of thing I love to do. Of course I'll come!"

My next move was to write and ask him about his choice of music and Scriptures to accompany his message. His answering letter dumbfounded me. He said, "Let's do it the other way around. You

tell me what your theme is and what songs and Scripture readings
you'd like, and God will help me fit my message into your plan." Talk
about a servant spirit. Talk about giving up the power of control! I
thought, *Here, in the flesh, is the kind of humility and flexibility that I
have been glimpsing in his writing.*

How well this man had been learning his own lessons! Nouwen
had lamented in *The Genesee Diary,*

> When I think of the many lecture invitations I declined
> with the argument that I had no time to prepare, I see now
> how I looked at every speaking engagement . . . as a new per-
> formance that calls for new preparation. . . . This attitude
> leads to fatigue and eventually to exhaustion. . . . Now I see
> that I was all mixed up, that I had fragmented my life into
> many sections that did not really form a unity. The question
> is not, "Do I have time to prepare?" but, "Do I live in a state
> of preparedness?"

And when we met the day before the conference was to begin,
he was as human and eager to please as a wise child. He showed me
some notes he'd jotted down; "Do you think this metaphor will work?
It's right out of my own life, but does it go well with the plans you've
made?" He kept coming back for my approval and even asked me to
pray with him about an idea he wanted to present. In the empty
chapel we sat there in the pew, and God was present in an almost
tangible way as this appealing but unassuming servant of God asked
humbly for help, for clarity of thought, for integrity, for the power of
the Spirit. And when the time came for him to speak, he was ignited
with that power. Love and wisdom streamed from him, and we were
powerfully affected for good.

And once again I gave thanks not only that our minds had intersected as I'd read his words on the printed page, but that when our
paths had crossed he had given me a living model of wisdom, grace,
and obedient servanthood that reminded me of Christ himself.

Four

Words Along the Way

by
John Mogabgab

Dear Chris:
. . . Keep me in your prayers as I continue my search for
wholeness and holiness. . . .

Henri Nouwen, June 4, 1988

John Mogabgab

John S. Mogabgab is the editor of *Weavings: A Journal of the Christian Spiritual Life*, published by the Upper Room in Nashville, Tennessee. Mr. Mogabgab is an Episcopal layperson with degrees in theology from Union Theological Seminary (New York) and Yale University. He has been a fellow of the Institute for Ecumenical and Cultural Research at St. John's University in Collegeville, Minnesota, and has served on the faculty of the Summer School Program in Theology at St. John's. He has been a consultant in spiritual growth for the Episcopal Diocese of Connecticut, a member of the advisory committee for the Annand Center for Spiritual Growth at Berkeley Divinity School at Yale University, a member of the leadership team and advisory board of the Academy for Spiritual Formation in Nashville, Tennessee, and an adjunct faculty member of McCormick Theological Seminary (Chicago), where he has taught in the Doctor of Ministry Program. He is a member of the Ecumenical Institute of Spirituality, a group of Protestant and Roman Catholic spiritual writers and retreat leaders founded by Douglas Steere, the noted Quaker spiritual leader, in response to Vatican II.

Mr. Mogabgab has led many retreats and workshops on the spiritual life. His articles and book reviews have appeared in *Reflection, Worship, Sojourners, The Thomist, Sisters Today*, and *The Interpreter*. Mr. Mogabgab is the principal author of the resource packet entitled *A New Heart, A New Spirit: Guidelines for Spiritual Growth in Parishes* (1984). He is a contributor to *Spirituality in Ecumenical Perspective* (1993) and is the editor of *The Weavings Reader: Living With God in the World* (1993) and *Communion, Community, Commonweal: Readings For Spiritual Leadership* (1995). Mr. Mogabgab enjoys hiking, canoeing, and wading rivers with fly rod in hand.

———————————

IN her autobiography, Annie Dillard recalls her encounters with the Bible at summer church school camp and weekly Sunday school: "Why did [the adult members of society] spread this scandalous document before our eyes? If they had read it, I thought, they would have hid it. They didn't recognize the vivid danger that we would, through repeated exposure, catch a case of its wild opposition to their world."[1] Significantly, the title of Dillard's autobiography is *An American Childhood*. She wants us to understand that for all their uniqueness, her younger years were also drenched in typically American activities and values, church attendance and Bible lessons among them. In another book, Dillard has this to say about Sunday worship:

> On the whole, I do not find Christians, outside of the catacombs, sufficiently sensible of conditions. Does anyone have the foggiest idea what sort of power we so blithely invoke?... It is madness to wear ladies' straw hats and velvet hats to church; we should all be wearing crash helmets. Ushers should issue life preservers and signal flares; they should lash us to our pews. For the sleeping god may wake someday and take offense, or the waking god may draw us out to where we can never return.[2]

When Henri Nouwen read and expounded the Bible, one began to sense the realities to which Annie Dillard points. During the five years I was Henri's research and teaching assistant at Yale, I had many opportunities to witness, in his encounters with God's Word, the power pulsing deep within the strange world of the Bible. There were times, especially when Henri's whole body would tense or tremble with the energy of a particular Scripture text, that I wished there had been a crash helmet within reach! Henri engaged everything with his whole being, and when it was the Bible that had his attention, I often experienced the low rumbling of deep calling to deep within the holy words I was hearing (Ps. 42:7). As Henri led us into the caverns and canyons of Scripture, we felt stirring within us a fresh yearning for the dangerous but kindly mystery of God. He awakened

---

1. Annie Dillard, *An American Childhood* (New York: Harper & Row, 1987), 134.
2. Annie Dillard, *Teaching A Stone To Talk* (New York: Harper & Row, 1982), 40–41.

me, as well as many others, from the amiable slumber Annie Dillard evokes with both gentle humor and urgent concern.

In Henri's presence the Bible became three-dimensional, and I slowly realized that for some time I had been gasping for air under the smothering, dull torment of banality. There seemed to have been a flattening of life that left little room for genuine novelty, bracing freshness, invigorating immediacy. For many people, work was being shorn of its larger meaning and dignity by the slow erosion of trust and fidelity between companies and their employees. Human relationships were becoming brittle and burdensome under the unforgiving scrutiny of self-interest. Violence and gross conduct were being transmuted into entertainment through the strange alchemy of talk shows and made-for-TV movies. Landscapes were being rendered faceless and whole ecosystems knocked senseless by human greed. In more than a few churches, people were feeling that they must dress up pretty for Jesus on Sunday morning and wait until Wednesday evening's Twelve-Step program to seek healing for their wounds.

My friendship with Henri showed me that the spiritual life is many things, but it is not banal. The spiritual life soars on the updrafts of mystery, shimmers with the light of unquenchable hope, stands fast with the rugged constancy of love. What we desire so ardently today is to be gathered up in awe, delivered from the swarm of daily preoccupations that bind us as surely as the Lilliputians bound Gulliver.

As I was preparing to write this meditation, I found myself turning to the older spiritual writers for insight into my theme. I do this often when faced with the next *Weavings* editorial. This time, however, I asked myself why I so consistently look to these early teachers for wisdom. The answer was swift and sure. When I read the ancients, I catch a glimpse of the power and mystery of God's Word that sets things in a new frame of reference. The great writers of our common Christian heritage, many of whom I met for the first time in the company of Henri, address my need to touch the hem of a reality that infinitely surpasses my own small world—a reality that nonetheless involves itself with that world quite exquisitely. Evelyn Underhill sounds the pitch with which I resonate when she writes, "A spiritual life is simply a life in which all that we do comes from the center, where we are anchored in God: a life soaked through and through by a sense of His reality and claim, and self-given to the great movement of His Will."[3]

A life saturated by a sense of God's reality and claim, and relinquished to the all-embracing movement of God's will—such a life comes about, in part, through repeated immersion in Scripture. Scripture is a sea of marvels from which our spiritual life slowly emerges to stand on the terra firma of the world; Scripture is an uncharted wilderness where cloud and fire may be our only guides. Seventh century writer Isaac of Nineveh describes the words of Scripture as "fiery things" of surpassing power which clothe the soul in "fear and trembling."[4] In scripture's oceanic depths and vast sear landscapes, we meet a reality that causes fear and trembling not only because of its unimaginable majesty but also because of its boundless solicitude.

The God portrayed in Scripture is a God who is always forming something out of nothing—stars and earth and sea, creatures of every shape and size, the fearfully and wonderfully framed dimensions of every human life (Ps. 139:14–15 NRSV). Yet God's involvement with inconceivably distant galaxies never eclipses God's longing for an intimate relationship with each of us. Having intricately woven the fabric of our being, God knows us by name and will never forget us (Isa. 44:21, 24; 49:15). God cherishes us, loves us with an everlasting love (Isa. 43:4; Jer. 31:3). Again and again, the Bible places us before a God self-given to our cause, a God who therefore desires above all else to fashion us into the pattern of our proper end. Third-century Bishop Irenaeus of Lyons gives expression to a central truth of Scripture when he writes: "The glory of God is the human being fully alive."

---

3. Evelyn Underhill, *The Spiritual Life* (Oxford: Oneworld, 1993), 27.
4. St. Isaac of Nineveh, *On Ascetical Life*, trans. Mary Hansburg (Crestwood, N.Y.: St. Vladimir Seminary Press, 1989), 72–73.

Perhaps it is this richly textured portrait of God's unflagging interest in us that prompted earlier spiritual writers to describe Scripture with images of plenty and nurture, images that signal the formative influence of Scripture in spiritual growth and maturity. Fourth-century author Ephraem of Syria remarked that while fields produce their harvest and then become bare, Scripture furnishes untold bounty for all who reap its fruits.[5] Peter of Celle, a twelfth-century Cistercian abbot, evokes with rich imagery the nurturing effects of reading Scripture:

> Reading is the soul's food, light, lamp, refuge, consolation, and the spice of every spiritual savor. It feeds the hungry, it illuminates the person sitting in darkness; to refugees from shipwreck or war it comes with bread. It comforts the contrite heart, it contains the passions of the body with the hope of reward. When temptations attack, it counters them with the teaching and example of the saints. By it those who have recovered from infirmity are made strong in battle. Prosperity is kept within bounds by its power, lest we glory in our good fortune. Adversity too is limited, lest we waver in it. . . . In the bread box of sacred reading are breads baked in an oven, breads roasted on a grill, or cooked in a frying pan, breads made with the first fruits and sprinkled with oil, and barley cakes. So, when this table is approached by people from any walk of life, age, sex, status or ability, they will all be filled with the refreshment that suits them.[6]

Equally impressive are the consequences of failing to dine daily at the banquet table of Scripture. In the following passage from the same Peter of Celle, I am substituting the words "life" and "Christian" for references to hermits and their cells.

---

5. St. Ephraem, "On The Transfiguration of Our Lord and God and Saviour Jesus Christ," in *The Sunday Sermons of the Great Fathers, Vol. II*, trans. and ed. M. F. Toal (Chicago: Henry Regnery Co., 1958), 44–45.

6. Peter of Celle, *Selected Works*, trans. Hugh Feiss, OSB (Kalamazoo, Mich.: Cistercian Publications, 1987), 135.

I consider a [life] without reading to be a hell without consolation, ... a prison without light, a tomb without a vent,
a ditch swarming with worms, a suffocating trap. A [life]
without reading is the empty house of which the gospel
speaks, where the nocturnal and noonday devils assault the
idle [Christian] with as many thrusts of useless and harmful
thoughts as there are hours and moments in the day and
night.[7]

A life bereft of Scripture is spiritually cramped and susceptible to
undesirable influences. This makes all the more compelling the
Bible's recurring invitations to receive its sustenance and give ourselves to its formative purpose: "Taste and see that the LORD is good"
(Ps. 34:8). "Let anyone who is thirsty come to me, and let the one
who believes in me drink" (John 7:37–38 NRSV). "Ho, everyone who
thirsts, come to the waters; and you that have no money, come, buy
and eat! Come, buy wine and milk without money and without price.
Why do you spend your money for that which is not bread, and your
labor for that which does not satisfy? Listen carefully to me, and eat
what is good, and delight yourselves in rich food. Incline your ear,
and come to me; listen, so that you may live" (Isa. 55:1–3 NRSV). Do
you hear the invitation? Drink the nectar of God's love, savor the
bread of God's word, listen to the voice of God's invitation, "so that
you may live."

Henri Nouwen lived abundantly and was gifted at leading others to the same source of abundance. He prepared me to recognize
and respond to the wisdom in this counsel from Isaac of Nineveh:
"Read the two Testaments which God has constituted for the knowledge of the whole world, so that by the power of his Divine Economy,
[the world] may be provided with food in every generation, and be
enveloped in wonder."[8]

---

7. Peter of Celle, *Selected Works*, 133–34.
8. St. Isaac of Nineveh, *On Ascetical Life*, 71.

Five

Which Way to God?

by
Timothy Jones

Dear Chris:
Many thanks for your letter. The first word that came to
my mind after reading it was the word: vocation. The
main question is: "What is your vocation?" It is crucial
that you keep asking God: "What do you want of me and
my family? How do you want us to live our lives? Where
do you want us to be?" You have to keep asking this every
day in your prayers with the growing desire to do what
God in his love calls you to do. Do not worry too much
about details. They will all fall into place once your heart
and mind are clear about what you most desire and what
is also God's deepest desire for you. I believe that our
deepest desire is always in accordance with God's love.
He has created that desire in us. . . .

Henri Nouwen, March 3, 1988

Timothy Jones

Timothy Jones is a writer, editor, and speaker. His specialty is prayer and the spiritual life. He is a M.Div. graduate of Princeton Theological Seminary. Timothy has edited books for Upper Room Books and was managing editor for Moorings, a Nashville-based division of the Ballantine Publishing Group. For almost six years, Timothy was an editor at *Christianity Today* magazine and for eight years was a pastor. He co-authored *The Saints Among Us* with pollster George Gallup Jr. He wrote *Celebration of Angels*, *The Art of Prayer*, and *21 Days to a Better Quiet Time with God*. His latest book is *Awake My Soul*. Timothy lives in the Nashville, Tennessee, area with his wife, Jill, and their three children.

HENRI *Nouwen*, I decided that spring day in 1979, *will have to wait.* I was just days from graduating from Princeton Theological Seminary. Whenever I thought about the pastoral work I was about to begin, I entertained, like most of my classmates, a mix of lofty dreams and anxious flashes of doubt. Already I was mapping out sermons, planning pastoral visits, reviewing my class notes on church administration. My heart raced ahead with curiosity and hope.

I had a more immediate, lighter task that warm day in May. An adult Sunday school class from my home church in California had sent me a $300 check for books. This is my chance, I thought, to stock up on reference tools. I had scrimped through seminary, marrying my last year, but now I had the means to fill gaps in my pastoral library. I had never felt such exhilarating freedom in a bookstore.

But what to get? As I stood amid the volumes on theology and church history crowding Princeton's Theological Book Agency, my interests quickly took a practical bent. Knowing I would soon be giving a weekly sermon made me scour the shelves for biblical commentaries and books on preaching. I wanted to stand tall—and prepared—in my pulpit.

Shuffling through the aisles, I also saw books by Henri Nouwen, a Dutch priest and professor whose name I had heard, whose books I had had nodding acquaintance with: *The Wounded Healer, Reaching Out, The Living Reminder*. Nouwen was already distinguishing himself for his accent on spirituality. Students and faculty made his books recommended reading.

But I passed them by.

No, I would walk out with arms piled high with resources of the greatest pragmatic value. I wanted tangible help for day-in, day-out ministering to the people who had just called me to be their pastor. And soon enough I began the work—in great earnest.

I was the sole paid staff of Germantown Brick Church of the Brethren, a Protestant congregation with Anabaptist roots tucked in the southwest corner of Virginia, not far from the Blue Ridge Mountains. The church had over two hundred members, and despite my relative youth (I was only twenty-three), the members welcomed me warmly. I threw myself into the work, preaching, visiting in homes and hospitals tirelessly, burying the dead, marrying the young. I went at it so intensely that I would not even take a day off. I just worked and worked. Until, that is, my wife, mother of our first newborn, insisted I take a day off every week. As tired as I was getting, it didn't take much convincing.

And increasingly, the hunger for other resources began to gnaw within. I had been trying dutifully to pray most mornings. And late-Saturday nights drove me to God as I looked ahead to standing before a congregation waiting for a word from on high. But as I worked, I began to realize how much I was in danger of joining the ranks of ministers who, as Nouwen wrote in *The Living Reminder*, "have many projects, plans, and appointments, but who have lost their heart somewhere in the midst of their activities."[1] I realized that ingenuity could carry me along only so far. Yes, things at the church were going well. Unlike many first pastorates, this was a happy situation for pastor and people. But a gut feeling in my soul told me that I could not keep giving out without taking in.

So I began to read.

And now, not surprisingly, I turned to Henri Nouwen in the way, as a seminarian, I had not. I opened his books realizing that I needed more than honed techniques or head knowledge. I needed to pray. I needed wisdom, not information. God was catalyzing an expectation that ministry could be born of something deeper, more profound.

And that recognition arose in me just at the right moment in my life, for I was about to make a move that would create in me a holy desperation, an anguished crying out that led to the most profound discovery of my ministry. It began when my wife and I were invited by a judicatory of our denomination to start a new church in the suburbs of Houston. We had been at Germantown Brick Church only four years. But the excitement of "church planting" beckoned us to move. Friends told us, "if anybody can do it, you two can." We pulled our U-Haul truck full of possessions out of our driveway. We

1. Henri Nouwen, *The Living Reminder* (New York: Seabury, 1977), 11.

were nervous, but eager for the challenge ahead. We were full of ideas, and . . . full of ourselves.

But almost as soon as we arrived, boomtown Houston went bust. The city's oil industry was about to dry up, with devastating consequences for the economy—and our assignment. People in our tiny, fledgling church moved out of state in search of jobs, depleting our ranks. After a year we realized that our venture was not going to meet expectations—not ours, not those of our financial supporters. I would often go running in the mornings along the bike trails of the Woodlands, the name of our suburb, to think and pray and get away; the profuse sweat of my jogs in the humid Gulf Coast heat seemed emblematic of our entire experience. My wife and I slogged through two more tough years before we resigned.

But during that time, Nouwen emerged again from among the many authors whose books lined the shelves of my office. What I had been discovering about prayer in Virginia became more than a matter of mere interest. It appeared as a lifeline thrown by one who also struggled, but who had found a type of solid ground, a place that I had not yet discovered. I was learning, and slowly moved by what I read, moved by circumstances and sheer grace, to cling to God.

Sometimes I ached when I came to God in prayer; sometimes I felt impatient with a God who seemed to be leading us too languidly through our Houston wilderness. But I felt as if I had no choice but to come to God to receive. And in the thick (and thin) of what felt like frontline ministry, Nouwen helped me find my truer identity as a pastor. What edged me toward despair, became, with Nouwen, a source of growth.

My journal entries from these years in the early eighties brim with passages I cribbed from his books, passages I would come back to again and again. Like this one from Nouwen's *Genesee Diary*:

> Reflecting on the last three years of work [in the world of academics and teaching], I realize more and more that it lacked unity. The many things I did during those years seemed disjointed, not really relating to each other, not coming from one source. I prayed during certain hours or

days but my prayers seemed separated from the lectures I gave, the trips I made, the counseling I did. When I think of the many lecture invitations I declined with the argument that I had no time to prepare, I see now how I looked at every speaking engagement—be it a lecture, a sermon or commencement address—as a new performance that calls for new preparation. As if I had to entertain a demanding audience that could not tolerate any poor performance. No wonder that this attitude leads to fatigue and eventually to exhaustion. . . . Now I see that I was all mixed up. . . . The question is not, "Do I have time to prepare?" but, "Do I live in a state of preparedness?"[2]

Ministry, I was coming to realize, is less what I do and more who I am becoming in Christ. Nouwen reminded me that I needed to do more than aim for profound sermons or effective pastoral calls. I needed a profound *life*, one made rich by the presence of God him-self. Amid the bustle, he nudged me to make unstinting room for spiritual realities. And when things went slower than I preferred, still, Nouwen seemed to say, God was present. I could watch things inch forward only to take big backward steps with something other than panic. I found the grace to trust that the entrance into God's kingdom is the result of a hidden but holy nature that grows out of our fumbling efforts.

Then I found another passage to drive the lesson home, a passage from *The Living Reminder* that also made its way into my journal, weaving into the fabric of my life and call:

In recent years, I have become more and more aware of my own tendency to think that the value of my presence depends on what I say or do. [*Yes,* I thought, *that's me, here in the laboring fields of Houston.*] And yet it is becoming clearer to me every day that this preoccupation with per-forming in fact prevents me from letting God speak through

2. Henri Nouwen, *The Genesee Diary* (Garden City, N.Y.: Doubleday, 1976), 59.

me in any way he wants, and so keeps me from making connections prior to any special word or deed. . . . Over the years
we have developed the idea that being present to people in
all their needs is our greatest and primary vocation. The
Bible does not seem to support this. Jesus' primary concern
was to be obedient to his Father, to live constantly in his
presence. Only then did it become clear to him what his task
was in his relationships with people.[3]

I never took this as a justification for passivity. I still worked
hard, but I saw that only in a relationship with God would I survive
when hopes fell flat. Nouwen kept pointing me not to specific tips
for ministry, but to the basis of all life and work. Look at Jesus,
Nouwen said in *Out of Solitude*. Here he is, not beginning the day as
most of us in ministry would—not with to-do lists and program
plans, but with a simple presence spent in the ultimate Presence:

In the middle of sentences loaded with action—healing suffering people, casting out devils, responding to impatient disciples, traveling from town to town and preaching from
synagogue to synagogue—we find these quiet words [in
Mark's gospel]: "In the morning, long before dawn, [Jesus]
got up and left the house, and went off to a lonely place and
prayed there." In the center of breathless activities we hear
a restful breathing. Surrounded by hours of moving we find
a moment of quiet stillness. . . . The more I read this nearly
silent sentence locked between the loud words of action, the
more I have the sense that the secret place of Jesus' ministry
is hidden in that lonely place where he went to pray, early
in the morning, long before dawn.[4]

I know that this was no facile step that Nouwen imagined he
had mastered. Nor did my reading what he said about prayer save
me from personal pain as our congregation slowly melted down.
But there was a difference in it all now. Someone was winsomely,

3. Nouwen, *The Living Reminder*, 30–31.
4. Henri Nouwen, *Out of Solitude* (Notre Dame, Ind.: Ave Maria, 1974), 13–14.

persuasively reminding me of what my soul already suspected and *longed* to believe.

People would often ask me, "How is your church doing?" (Or more bluntly, "How many people come to your worship services?") But inwardly I was working on more critical questions that were unsettling but ultimately more satisfying: "How is my prayer life?" "What does it mean to seek first the kingdom of God?" Questions like that were helping me find myself as a minister.

But at the same time, in one of those odd turns in a person's life I could never foresee, I also began to find my identity as a writer. I soon felt a subtle shift in the center of my vocation.

From Texas I went on to join a pastoral staff at a church in Indiana and, perhaps as significantly, worked half-time researching and writing the detailed centennial history of a denominational college an hour from our small Hoosier town. I was writing articles for denominational publications too, and I found my focus of interest shifting from the pulpit to the writer's desk.

I began reading books about writing. I took writing classes at a community college. When a magazine in the Chicago area, *Christianity Today*, offered to take me on as an assistant editor, the way seemed clear for a change.

Quickly my focus moved from juggling the daily demands of pastoring to negotiating printer's deadlines, relating to authors, dreaming up article ideas. And again by grace, I found myself unable to forget Nouwen. I did some translating of his ministry insights for my new setting, in a way. But Nouwen, the quintessential pastor, could still speak to me when I joined the ranks of those who pull down nine-to-five office jobs. With all my delight in my new vocational direction, still I asked, "How can I stay aware of God on the job?" And still Nouwen could help.

Nouwen proposed a simple way of prayer, using short, reverent phrases. This approach to spiritual life, he wrote in *The Way of the Heart*:

When we are faithful to it and practice it at regular times, slowly leads us to an experience of rest and opens us to God's active presence. Moreover, we can take this prayer with us into a very busy day. When, for instance, we have spent twenty minutes in the early morning sitting in the presence of God with the words, "The Lord is my Shepherd," they may slowly build a little nest for themselves in our heart and stay there for the rest of our busy day. Even while we are talking, studying, gardening, or building [or editing], the prayer can continue in our heart and keep us aware of God's ever-present guidance.[5]

So I tried. I didn't always manage to have regular prayer times (or random prayer times, for that matter). I suspect Nouwen didn't either. But I knew I could not neglect this spiritual subterranean spring, even when I came to my quiet times groggy-eyed and antsy to get to my desk.

And as I worked with words, I found Nouwen reminding me, yet again, to find the substance beneath the turns of phrase and artful article titles we strove for at our editorial office. Nouwen learned before I did that while words carry great weight, they also come with severe limitations. And in prayer they matter less than we usually think.

I found a new freedom in prayer, a new simplicity. After hours of struggling to find the perfect combinations of words for the articles I wrote or edited, I could simply concentrate on the heart's inchoate, sometimes mumbling utterances. Himself drawing on another spiritual teacher, a desert father, Nouwen pointed me to seventh-century monk John Climacus: "When you pray do not try to express yourself in fancy words," John Climacus said, "for often it is the simple, repetitious phrases of a little child that our Father in heaven finds most irresistible. Do not strive for verbosity lest your mind be distracted from devotion by a search for words. . . . When you find satisfaction or compunction in a certain word of your prayer, stop at that point." Concluded Nouwen, "This is a very helpful suggestion for us, people who depend so much on verbal ability."[6] He could have been writing for me, as I now suspect he was writing for himself.

---

5. Henri Nouwen, *The Way of the Heart* (New York: Seabury, 1981), 82.
6. Nouwen, *The Way of the Heart*, 81.

As I had hoped and prayed, my years of editing led to increasing opportunities to write. I began to pen books that publishers wanted to buy, on a subject that crystallized as central to my vocation: the spiritual life. I soon found myself with more writing projects than I could handle in the margins around a full-time job, especially after a brief stint as managing editor for an imprint of a major New York publisher. So dreams of devoting my work time to writing congealed.

And Nouwen, once again, gently prodded me to one of the key lessons any writer must lean toward: Let God speak through me and my own story, with all my warts and foibles. Nouwen emphatically encouraged me to be vulnerable in what I wrote. He did it in his writing by never acting like he had arrived. Especially from his published journals, *The Genesee Diary*, *The Road to Daybreak*, but elsewhere too, the struggle was never far from view. I took mental notes as I read.

One day at the office of *Christianity Today*, then-acting editor-in-chief Harold Myra told me of his meeting Nouwen at an airport lounge, years before. Nouwen had flown in for an interview for a sister publication for pastors. Nouwen, Myra recounted, spoke with a poignant, moving honesty. He told Myra of a recent experience that seemed akin to a breakdown. And Nouwen did not flinch in telling it. Indeed, in his authenticity and transparency he used it as a kind of object lesson. "These past months I've come face to face with my own spiritual abyss," he said in the interview that was eventually published in *Leadership* journal. Later in the interview Nouwen concluded, "One of the most beautiful ways for spiritual direction to take place is to let your insecurity lead you closer to the Lord.... In a sense, you let your psychological trembling become trembling for the Lord."[7] Myra was moved by such unself-conscious authenticity. So was I.

Recently, flipping through *The Art of Prayer*, which I wrote a couple of years ago, I realized how much Nouwen had taught me, without my knowing it. I shared my struggles with an honesty I don't think I would have had the courage for if someone had not modeled it first. I saw themes that have become my own, but largely because I encountered them first through Nouwen's transparent writing. I

---

7. Henri Nouwen, "Deepening Our Conversation with God," *Leadership* (1982, vol. xx).

knew I had permission to speak not as a spiritual genius but as a soul who was simply, imperfectly seeking God.

If Nouwen, without knowing it, taught me much of what I know about pastoring or writing, I find his insights guiding me around what may be yet another vocational bend in the road. My interest in nurturing prayer and spirituality, fed all these years by Nouwen and others like him, seems to be coming full circle. As a result I have begun exploring ordination in my new denominational home, the Episcopal Church. In many ways I have never not been a pastor, even these past years in which I have held an office job or closeted myself in my writer's study. But now I feel ready again to make that pastoral work more explicit, through what I write, through the workshops I lead, through the congregants I may labor among.

Where it will lead, I cannot say for certain. But Nouwen provides me yet again with a vocabulary and a model that spur me on. This time the teaching has come not through a book, but from a personal encounter Nouwen had with someone I know. Here is how I heard it:

I was seated at the dinner table last year, when Abram, my oldest son, working to save money for college by painting houses, told me of a conversation from his day at work. His boss's wife had learned of my interest in prayer, had seen something I wrote where I had quoted Nouwen. And she said, "I know who Nouwen is!" And this is the story she told in response:

Louise, I'll call her, had been almost dragged to a talk Nouwen was giving in Nashville. Her friend had wanted to do something with Louise that evening, and Louise was thinking that going out for drinks suited her better than hearing a priest lecture. But her friend prevailed, and they sat through Nouwen's two-hour talk. By now Louise was really ready to go. But her friend again insisted on something else: She wanted Nouwen to sign her copy of a book of his she had just bought. The two waited in a long line, got the book signed, turned to go, and then, out of the blue, Nouwen took Louise's hand. He told her simply, gently, "You are a special child of God." Just like that. It was an unexpected grace, a wonderfully odd encounter. And a message she needed desperately to hear. She hasn't been quite the same since.

And I think, *this is ministry*. This is what people need to hear. Whether I preach it, quietly live it, or write about it, this is what the world longs to know, what I need to convey. And what I need continuously to learn.

I never met Henri Nouwen, or saw him in person, even from afar. But he still imparts a quiet wealth to me through what he wrote, what he did, how he lived. At every turn, it seems, Nouwen has had a way of reminding me of what truly matters to the human soul. And so his ministry lives quietly on.

Six

In the Journey, We Need Friends

by
Fred Rogers

Dear Chris:
. . . I do not know Fred Rogers but I met his very kind
wife when she accepted the Christopher Award in New
York in his name. . . .

Henri Nouwen, November 23, 1984

Fred Rogers

F red Rogers is a husband, father, grandfather, a graduate of Rollins College with a degree in music composition, an ordained minister in the United Presbyterian Church, and the creator of the Emmy Award-winning children's television program on PBS: *Mister Rogers' Neighborhood.*

ONCE in a while when the phone rings at home in the evening, I think, "Maybe that's Henri," but of course it isn't because Henri is in heaven now. I miss his calls.

He must have had huge phone bills because he'd call us—his friends—from all over the world. He'd usually start out by saying, "Hello, Fred. This is Henri." In fact, he'd talk so quickly it most often sounded like, "Hello, Fred . . . Henri." I'd ask him where he was, and he'd say Toronto or Holland or Russia or California or England or Santa Fe, but then he'd get right to his point: *"How are you?"* He always wanted to know how *I* was. When my best friend from high school was dying, Henri would invariably ask, "And how is Jim doing?" He'd even call Jim and his wife and ask *them*, "How are you?" And he really wanted to know. He wanted to be connected with all of us in the most essential ways.

The first time I met Henri, Chris de Vinck took me to Harvard to visit at his "house" there. We weren't there very long before Henri said, "It's time for prayers. Won't you join us?" So before we knew it, a few of us were climbing the stairs to a little room (an upper room) where we got down on little wooden kneelers and all of us read the lesson of the day. Henri was so much at home on those little kneelers as he was in the classroom or the writing office—or on the phone.

Henri was in touch—in communion—with the Essential of life. It wasn't hard to recognize that he was in an enthusiastic relationship with God . . . in all that he felt and did.

"Words, words, words," he'd say. "They're everywhere! On billboards, on television screens, in newspapers and books. . . ." He spoke about how many words lost their power, yet words like "I love you" (said from the heart) are still able to "give another person new life, new hope, new courage." Well, it seems that even in his death, Henri continues to say not only "How are you?" but "I love you"—now through an earthly silence.

In fact, Henri's death has confirmed for me the enormous power of silence. Even though most of the world knows Henri best by his words, I've come to recognize his deepest respect for the still, small voice among the quiet of eternity. That's what continues to inspire me.

Each morning I pray for my family and my friends—by name. When I come to Henri's name, I look at his photo on the back of his "Adam" book, and I put my fingers on his sweater and I say, "Thank you." When I go swimming each day, just before I jump into the pool, I sing to myself the Taizé "Jubilate Deo." Henri taught it to us at the table at L'Arche Daybreak. When I meet with teenagers, I often teach them the round, "Ubi caritas et amor . . . Deus ibi est," ("Wherever charity and love reside . . . there is God") another gift from Henri. Henri offered us things in such a natural way that he made it seem like "nothing" to pass them on. "Well, of course you can do that," Henri always seems to be saying.

One time in Boston, some Roman Catholic friends and I were invited to meet the bishop. Henri wasn't with us. During our visit, the bishop brought us to his chapel, and he offered Mass. When it came time for the Eucharist, I stepped up right along with my friends. (Henri always included me in his Mass.) I had my hand outstretched to receive the Communion, but the bishop gently, but firmly, put down my hand and simply made the sign of the Cross on my forehead. I was the only one in the room who didn't receive the host.

Henri had a view of God—of Jesus—(of everything) that reflected what Martin Luther King Jr. often said: "The universe is under control of a Loving Purpose." God knows how to help us feel welcomed, accepted, loved. Henri knew how too. And now he does it in that great, loving silence of the universe.

Instead of any more words, I'd like to give you, the reader, some silence to use for your own reflection—perhaps about Henri, perhaps about someone else who has helped you to see beyond the obvious, someone who has encouraged you to grow into a thoughtful person who cares about the essentials of life—perhaps a person who, like Henri and many of us, longs for deep friendships and reaches out to others in response to that longing—just as our God reached out through Jesus the Christ our Lord.

"How are you?" asks Henri.

"How are you?" Asks Jesus.

"I love you, as you are."
May your moment of silence bring you real peace.
Alleluia, Alleluia in laetitia!

Amen.

Seven

Traveling Without a Map

by
Andy Drietcer

Dear Chris:
. . . Please keep me in your prayers as I teach at Har-
vard. Pray that I may speak words that reach the heart of
people who are crying out for a new spiritual life. . . .
                              Henri Nouwen, March 14, 1984

Andy Drietcer

Andrew Drietcer is the father of ten- and eight-year-old daughters and the husband of Wendy, with whom he is part-time co-pastor of Sleepy Hollow Presbyterian Church in San Anselmo, California. Raised in rural Indiana, he studied religion at Wabash College, Oxford University, and Yale Divinity School, lived for a year at the French Community of Taizé, and holds a Ph.D. in Christian Spirituality from the Graduate Theological Union, Berkeley. In addition to serving as a pastor, Andy teaches at San Francisco Theological Seminary, where he is Director of the Graduate Certificate in the Art of Spiritual Direction and Co-Director of the Youth Ministry and Spirituality Project. He's hoping to become a piano-playing carpenter in the second half of his life.

I WAS eating my lunch. Chatting with friends. Lois walked by and stopped at my elbow. Her interruption wasn't exactly annoying, but it seemed pointless: "Hey, you going to Henri's meeting?"

"What meeting?"

"You know, to interview for his course."

"Lois, what's the point? Henri's not going to let me in. Why should he? It's a *spiritual direction* course. It's not for people who think they don't believe in God."

"Oh, come with me anyway. What do you have to lose? Going to the meeting won't hurt anything. Henri won't mind. And it's always worthwhile hearing what he has to say."

Reluctantly, I followed her—lunch unfinished.

The meeting was in the small balcony room overlooking the Yale Divinity School Refectory. I crept in behind Lois, still hungry, feeling like an interloper, a fraud—especially when I noticed that most of those gathered around the table were the most "spiritual" students at the divinity school. Henri had called this meeting at the end of the spring semester after announcing that the coming year would be his last at Yale. He was preparing to offer a spiritual direction course that would be limited to twelve students. Suspecting he would be swamped with requests for admission, Henri was using this gathering as a way to give information about the course, to respond to questions, and to identify persons who might match the tenor of the class.

My fears about the meeting were justified. In my insecurity about my own lack of a spiritual life, all I heard from students were comments that seemed to me to advertise the holiness of the speakers. Feeling more and more threatened, exasperated, convinced I would never match the requirements for admission to this class, I finally blurted out, "What if you don't believe you have a spirit to direct? Can you be in a spiritual direction course?"

My question rose out of years of interior struggles, struggles that were masked by a seemingly faithful, unquestioning adherence to the tradition handed down to me. Ahead of me ran four generations of Presbyterian ministers. My maternal grandfather, in the second of these generations, was the pastor of the church I grew up in. With

David Niven looks and a Walter Cronkite voice, my grandfather preached a gospel of solid, Midwestern piety and progressive social justice in Wabash, Indiana, for thirty years. From my earliest years, my grandfather quizzed me after each worship service: "So, what was the sermon about today?" Eager to gain the favor of this saintly figure, I delighted in being able to demonstrate how closely I'd been listening, to prove how well I understood. I do not know what his motives were in the asking, but certainly his attention formed in me, his oldest grandchild, the foundations for a life of theological inquiry, the seeds of a constant search for a sense of the presence of God.

By the time I reached my teen years, my grandfather had retired. Then he died. His legacy to me: at thirteen years of age, I was at ease with historical-critical perspectives on Scripture and liberal Christian involvement in social issues. For better and for worse, these matched my critical (even cynical) teenage sensibilities. But these sensibilities left me unprepared for the charismatic movement that began seeping into our church at the beginning of the 1970s. The grand God of the social gospel presented by my grandfather was being replaced by a small, sticky-sweet god, a candy-coated deity that offered a little spiritual pick-me-up, a brightener, a sweet charge, whenever you needed it. I wasn't buying it.

Whatever teenage cynicism I directed toward Christianity was magnified during these years of encountering this particular brand of charismatic evangelicalism. Its biblical literalism offended my intellect. Its individualism offended my understanding that Christianity was about transforming the world. Its saccharine piety offended my sense that the Christian faith was about much more than merely feeling good. And its prayer life offended my conviction that God was not a magician. If this were Christianity, I thought, only idiots and narcissists could be Christians.

I sought viable alternatives. I found none. I did not appreciate the faithfulness alive in my own family. The style of church I grew up with no longer attracted me. Instead of supporting spiritual life, it seemed to be sinking in spiritual lifelessness. The heirs of the form of Christianity represented by my grandfather were committed to social change—a commitment I deeply admired—but I could not find the presence of God in the Christian life they espoused.

God was distant, out of touch, concerned only with grand issues of right and wrong, issues of justice. But we could never really *feel* God's concern. God stayed impersonal, expecting us to solve our own problems, soothe our fears, support our lives, change our world, right the wrongs by ourselves. The god of my charismatic, evangelical acquaintances could be called upon to work magical changes in my life and in the life of others, but this god of social change did not respond to prayers at all. People prayed, of course, but was there a point?

My discouragement was not eased when I read Dietrich Bonhoeffer's *The Cost of Discipleship*. Here was a third way, a Christianity totally committed to living intimately with God in the way of Christ, serving others to the point of death, and changing the world in the process. Surely, the Christian life must be lived like this or not at all. But no one I knew lived the way of Bonhoeffer's discipleship. Certainly I was not capable of such commitment.

So, for a decade I was caught between three forms of Christianity I could not embrace: first, an individualistic, literalistic pietism devoted to a tiny, sweet, magical God; second, a liberal intellectualism committed to the idea of a just God, and intimate with no god at all; third, a costly discipleship that seemed impossible to live out and evoked in me more guilt than freedom.

During the first years of this period I played the faithful Christian teenager, attending church and youth group weekly, studying and memorizing Bible passages, and discussing issues of faith with anyone who seemed interested. I lived an exemplary teenage life, excelling in sports, leading my high school class in scholarship, and winning community awards and respect for leadership beyond the classroom. Then on to a first-rate college, achieving academic honors as a religion major, assisting a minister in a small country church, going under care of my presbytery for ordination, being admitted to Yale Divinity School intent on a career teaching systematic theology.

At divinity school I reveled in theology courses, attended chapel daily, worked on issues of peace and justice, enjoyed and endured the wonders and pains of romantic relationships, immersed myself in the poverty and abundance of student life, and participated each afternoon in Henri's Eucharist service in the prayer chapel. Throughout these years I hid the thing that motivated my veneer of faithful, successful living: I longed for God, for a true presence of God within me. In fact, this longing gradually turned to desperation. If I had no sense of God in my life, what was the point?

From this growing desperation had come my question to Henri: "What if you don't believe there is a spirit to direct?"

If Henri heard my question and answered it in that meeting, I don't remember what he said. I was never really sure that Henri heard *anything* I said to him. His answers always responded to what I had *not* said—the unspoken heart of the matter. True to form, Henri's real answer came several days after the meeting: my name appeared on the list of those admitted to his class.

That autumn twelve of us gathered for Henri's course in spiritual direction. I should not have been surprised when I heard each of the other students admitting to a version of the quiet desperation that chilled the center of my own life. The format of the class was quite simple. One day each week of the semester we spent five hours at a retreat center on the Connecticut shoreline. After guiding us in a time of gathering and centering, Henri read aloud a Scripture passage and interpreted it in a way that led us to look more deeply at our lives with God. Then we spent extended time alone—meditating on what we had heard, walking on the beach, watching tiny crabs in the tide pools, contemplating flowers in the garden, napping, praying in the chapel with the day's Scripture passage—before gathering for a period of group silence and an opportunity to share our experiences.

I was not easily drawn into this process. By the time the course began, my desperation was filled with visions of suicide. I had stopped riding my bicycle for fear of "accidentally" turning into an oncoming car. I avoided walking on bridges. I visited a psychologist, who decided I was afraid of being drafted and of dying in a war. At the time there was no war. There was no draft. I abandoned psychology and suffered in secret. I threw myself into my studies and my work. But the more I excelled, the more I accomplished, the more meaningless my life seemed.

If God did not exist—and I had no inkling of anything to the contrary—neither living nor dying had a point. My life felt so meaningless I couldn't even move to end it. This sense of apathetic inaction helped keep me alive, as did the thought that as long as I was alive one more day there was some possibility of finding God. I clung desperately to the slippery hope that someone or something might throw me a lifeline.

It would be handy to be able to say that at some point in his spiritual direction course Henri said something that changed my life, revealed God to me, saved me. But it was not to be. Henri's gift was more subtle, more complex than that. Henri was the companion that kept pointing me, with the rest of the class, in a direction I had never gone. He'd been on this path for quite a while—at least longer than we had—and now he was accompanying this rag-tag group of desperate almost-believers.

At different points on the path he drew our attention to new sites, stopped with us to savor new experiences. And it was clear to all of us that Henri was seeing new things along the way, as well. They were new to him because he was seeing them from our fresh perspectives. As we described what we saw, Henri helped us interpret them or told what they looked like to him or shared the perspectives of those faithful Christians who had gone before us. And always he seemed to behold our experiences with childlike wonder. In other words, we learned about spiritual direction primarily because Henri modeled it for us. He showed us how to be the spiritual friend, the sacred companion. He offered us the space and time to be companions to one another.

An essential part of Henri's sacred companionship was the environment of encouragement he formed around us. For me, the critical piece of that environment was his requirement that we seek out an individual spiritual director. Resistant to the end, I decided my spiritual director would be a systematic theology professor with no spiritual direction experience. Once again Henri surprised me: "It will be good for both of you," he said, head cocked, shirt-tail out, peering through his glasses with a mischievous smile. How did he know that it would be in my meetings with my spiritual director that my new spiritual life would begin to form most clearly? In the midst of the fears and insecurities he wrote about so eloquently, Henri had an incredible capacity to trust that the Spirit of God would emerge in unexpected places.

I met with my spiritual director weekly. I did not want to talk about my prayer life, my sense of God's presence in the details of my life, or anything else that I thought might be the territory of the spiritual direction relationship. Instead, I wanted information. I wanted alternatives. I needed somebody to lay out descriptions of a God to whom I might be able to relate. So I asked questions, a question per week. And each week the answers I received proved nothing, convinced me of nothing. Instead, they showed me the limitations of the versions of God I thought I was required to believe in. They knocked down the false gods I had constructed out of the pieces of truth I'd grasped. They showed me I didn't need to conform to someone else's life with Christ. Rather, my own version of life with Christ was good enough—even good enough to be treasured by the God I sought, the God who would not let me go.

After about six weeks of theology-filled spiritual direction meetings, I realized that I had two questions left. I began to suspect that if my spiritual director could give me solid answers to these questions, I could believe in the existence of God. In fact, that is what came to pass. Over the course of two more meetings, my spiritual director answered my questions in ways that satisfied my longings.

My first question had to do with God's size. In spite of all the theology I had read relating to this question, I was not convinced there was a legitimate Christian image of divinity that offered a God big enough to invest my life in. My spiritual director wasted no time disabusing me of that notion. He offered me the image of an expansive Christian God. But more than that, he gave me permission to accept such a God, a God who is the grounding of all things, moving in and through all things, the Presence in which we and all creation "live and move and have our being" (Acts 17:28). Yes, this God was big enough for me. This God was big enough to handle the universe and more.

But how could such a universe-encompassing God be personally involved in caring for *my* life? How could *I* matter to such a God? How could *anybody* matter to such a God? My spiritual director helped me consider this possibility: the God of Scripture, the God who comes to us in Christ, is not simply personal, but "supra-personal." Unfortunately, our tendency is to define "personal" according to what we know of our relationships with persons. In these interpersonal relationships there is always an uncrossable boundary between individuals. But God is more than personal. This expansive God in whom we have our being is closer to us than we are to ourselves. God knows us better than we know ourselves. Our problem is that this supra-personal God is so close to us, in and through us, that we have difficulty identifying what parts of our lives are God and which are bits of us. God is so close to us that we often miss God's presence with us. So close that we often miss the Christ in us and in the people we know and meet. So close that we often miss the presence of the Spirit in the world around us. God is that intimate.

As I consider these questions now, I know that the answers I received are not earthshaking—but they did shake my own life free from the intellectual box that trapped it. In fact, the day I asked my final question, I had entered my spiritual director's office still at the edge of suicide; an hour later I left full of unspeakable relief and a growing sense of joyful trust that God loves me. That sense of fundamental trust has stayed with me now for almost two decades. It has fueled my commitments. It has given me a heart that can seek God's realm on earth with God, not on my own. It has offered me the hope that anything is possible—even freedom from my self.

Two things flowed immediately from this newfound freedom. First, I decided that my life needed to be formed in light of the mysterious, intimate God I was beginning to glimpse. So, Henri's spiritual direction course took on new significance for me. While my relationship with my spiritual director soon dwindled away, the class time became a chance to enter into the experience of a new way of being with God. Meditating at the tide pools, the Scripture reading, the shared reflections, the silence, all these began to form in me a sensibility for God's presence. Further, out of that growing longing for deeper spiritual formation I arranged to spend my seminary intern year at the Community of Taizé in France. That year of contemplative living continues to shape my life.

The second result of my new sense of freedom was an enduring shift in the question that fueled my intellectual pursuits and my sense of call to ministry. No longer did I ask, "Does God exist?" Now I began to ask, "Where do I meet God?" The answer: God is greeting me in all parts of my life; in the most usual, daily, ordinary pieces, in my supervisor at work and in the sunset and in my neighbor and in the county planning department and in my wife and in every place else in the world.

Yes, that was the answer I formed during that time of finding God at Yale. I believe it was more than merely an academic formulation. In fact, it fueled my further studies in Christian spirituality and led to my work directing a program for the development of spiritual directors. But it wasn't until almost a decade later that I truly came to taste some of what Henri longed for all of us to savor. In the midst of my doctoral studies and my wife's hectic pastoral ministry, Hannah was born, and then Monica. Wendy and I entered the "lost years" of parenthood, sleepless nights followed by days of mental haze. In those endless nights something extraordinary happened. As I sat in the cold darkness, wrapped in blankets, a tiny child held to my chest, rocking and softly humming, my times of praying in Henri's course came back to me—but in a new way. I began to imagine that I too was being rocked, held in the arms of God, warm and secure and loved. And who was this in my arms but God's own child, in whose face shone holy light. Each night I sank into this circle of holding divine love and being held by divine love. Each night I beheld the wonder of the God of Jesus, the Mystery to which Henri had pointed me.

Henri's companionship had prepared me to look at life with new eyes, with a certain attentiveness, with a certain expectation. From this new vantage point, I began to see the look, hear the voice, feel the activity of something that just might be the ripples of the presence of God. I began to touch the God who waits for me, longs for me and hopes that I will meet Christ in every part of my life, every dimension of this world.

This is the life that Henri helped free in me as he accompanied me on a piece of my journey. And as I minister to people in a small congregation and to persons who come from around the country to be formed in the spiritual direction program I oversee, I have come to realize ever more fully that my spiritual hunger is not mine alone. I share it with so many folks in this world.

Those many years ago I went hungry to a meeting with Henri Nouwen. And in his company I was—with so many others—fed the Bread of Life.

Eight

Our Hope on the Journey

by
Kelly Monroe

Dear Chris:
. . . After much thought I have decided to leave Harvard.
It simply was not the right place for me. I am going for a
year to France to study, read, write, and pray. I found a
small office for mail at the Maryknoll house in Cam-
bridge. That will be my U.S.A. base while I am in
Europe. The future is open-ended. I do not know yet
where I will settle eventually, but we will see. God will let
me know when I need to know. . . .

Henri Nouwen, June 3, 1985

Kelly Monroe

Kelly Monroe is the founder of the Harvard Veritas Forum and the advisor to the National Veritas Forum, which has emerged in more than seventy secular universities as a creative and "symphonic" exploration of Truth in relation to Jesus Christ. She edited and wrote *Finding God at Harvard* while working with the Graduate School Christian Fellowship.

Kelly loves sports, especially ultimate Frisbee, skiing, and squash. And her happiest times are camping or on the farm with family and friends, especially little ones discovering eggs in the chicken coop or milk in the cows.

The only thing that counts is faith expressing itself through love.
Galatians 5:6

HENRI Nouwen did not teach in the modern and banal sense. Rather, he sought to invite his students at Harvard Divinity School into the wonderful presence of Jesus through prayer, Scripture, solitude, Sabbath meals, and worship together—no matter how countercultural this was at Harvard.

Perhaps Nouwen's vulnerable spirit is offensive in a place like Harvard and to people like me—he shakes our attempts to construct successful, competitive, and impermeable selves. But in truth, who can condemn Nouwen's teaching? He lived as one who is meek and poor in spirit, as one who mourns. He recognized that he was shipwrecked and in need of salvation (see *The Way of the Heart*). He was, in spirit and deed, a wounded healer.

Henri taught that central to prayer is intimacy with God who is our wellspring of life and joy. In this state of prayer, he suggested, we are like the prodigal son whose homecoming is in the true shelter of his father's arms. Contentment, he believed, is "to be held."

Henri was concrete in his expression of faith, hope, and love. Harvard, on the other hand, is more interested in the "big picture" (and helping to paint the big picture). This big picture is an abstraction in which ideologies seem more important than actual people, reducing them in human and binary logic to mere statistics. In the words of poet-farmer Wendell Berry, "Abstraction is always the enemy."

Henri was interested in living a million small and concrete kindnesses: eyes filled with light and attention; ears quick to hear; feet and hands eager to serve. He modeled fellowship over competition. He offered the light of life over the heat of self-asserting ideas.

Sometimes it is difficult to know the difference between being "gifted" and being "handicapped." Do the gifted know that they are the Father's beloved? Do the gifted know to seek mercy so that they are free to love? Do the gifted see more than others do? Is God pleased with the skeptical intellect of a worldly scholar or with the wide-eyed soul of a humble child? Does the gift of knowledge or the gift of wisdom matter to God? Information or transformation? High scores on moral reasoning exams or the good heart bearing the fruit of a small and quiet kindness?

In *The Road to Daybreak*, Henri compassionately shared his view that Harvard Divinity School was inhospitable to Jesus and "thoroughly secular." He was eventually led out of this "desert" to be with mentally handicapped adults at L'Arche in Toronto.

I arrived in Cambridge the year after Henri left. While writing my thesis, and later while working with the Grad Student Christian Fellowship at Harvard, I considered myself too busy to read any of Nouwen's insights into Sabbath, solitude, prayer, listening, attention, and obedience in which we are broken and blessed in order to serve. Nor did I come to really know myself, in the Father's heart, as "beloved." ("I know I agree with Henri," thought I. "So why bother reading him? Why spend time in the sanctuary when I could be in the parking lot, waving new folks in?" And so went my foolish logic.)

For years, while running nearly on empty, I was busy taking on the world for the cause of Christ and doing "big things" for God. But while I was speaking of *Veritas* (truth), Nouwen was quietly living in truth, moment by moment, quietly and meekly, authentically and deeply. I cared much about holding truth, but the Person of Truth cared more about holding me. He wanted me to rest in him as his beloved child. He wanted me to be in him before doing anything. But I did not hear.

Now I wonder what would have happened if I had slowed down in order to read and to really hear Henri Nouwen (or Jesus' sermon on the mount, the Gospels, and Proverbs). What was the cost of my ignorance and distraction and obfuscation? What did Mary know that her sister Martha did not know? What really are "first things"? How would it have changed my life if I had rested in Christ and had heard his voice before my life was stunned to a stop by personal loss? What if I had ignored life's distractions and listened instead to my own heart? What if I had asked Jesus to heal and refuel me, to fill me with himself, so that I was not too exhausted to really love another person?

Had I received Henri's wisdom earlier, I believe that I would not have lost the dearest friend to my heart, the one I yearned to marry, the one with whom I had hoped to live, and serve, each day of my life.

While I was waiting for this friend to hear God's will, so obvious to me, and to solidify his commitment, he was waiting for me to have a hearing heart, to focus, and to enter with him into the intimate love of our Father. Every distraction pulled us out of the sanctuary. Had I read Nouwen, had I cultivated a deep heart of prayer, I might have put down some of my projects (which seemed so crucial, in my small brain, to advance the Gospel). Hearing the truth, I might have reached beyond my fears and activities and loved with abandon this man who gave so much to me. I might have presumed less, and seen, heard, and loved more.

I was busy, for example, helping to begin a movement affecting many universities that this friend and I called the Veritas Forum (which is a symphonic way to explore Truth in relation to Jesus). Had I read Nouwen's books I might have stopped reacting to the telephone and the Internet every time new friends asked for help at Stanford and Yale, Berkeley and West Point, Canada and Brazil, and dozens of other schools. If I had read Henri's words, I might have respected God's boundaries of time and space and seasons in my life. I might have learned balance, prudence, self-control, and the wisdom of Mary who chose the better path by first sitting at the feet of Jesus. I might have better bloomed where I was planted.

If I had allowed the writings of Henri Nouwen into my life sooner, I might have reprioritized the urgency to finish our book for publication, "the book" of journeys that we hoped would lead many to Christ. (Henri regretted not being able to write for the book: he was called to be with friends at L'Arche.)

The devil has a way of turning good intentions into exhausting battles. At times I became a crusader who could get lost in issues and discussions about social justice, homosexuality and gender, or "irreducible complexity" in molecules and cells (a theory of Michael Behe's which brilliantly challenges the error of Darwinism). We explored the likeness and relevance of modern cosmology to the biblical story of creation. We welcomed dozens of alumni and guests, such as John Stott, Os Guinness, Ron Sider, and Tony Campolo, to speak on the wholeness of the Gospel as good news for all creation, especially the poor. As the lives of students were threatened by the tragic myth of free sex, we tried to reveal the beauty of Scripture's teaching on the human body and on sexuality within the covenant of marriage. (All this work exhausted me more and more, at the expense of such a marriage to model myself.)

Thanks to leaders like Jeffrey Barneson and many wonderful students, our Christian fellowship was like coals gathered for a fire to offer light and warmth. Rather than arguing about the superiority of Christianity over other world religions and worldviews, we tried to put forth a light so lovely that all would be drawn into the presence of Jesus. We were gutsy, sometimes smart, and once in a blue moon effective.

We invited Harvard administrators to discuss the college's responsibility to its spiritual heritage. (Harvard was founded in 1636 "for Christ's glory.") I joined students serving poor Latin American friends during summers. I helped other friends battle against apartheid in South Africa and against persecution of African Christians in Sudan. We cared about truth, goodness, and beauty. In general, we did good stuff.

But in all that busyness, I neglected to care better for my neighbor, to love more completely the man to whom I was called. Why did I not go away alone for even three days to seek to know God's heart, my heart, and my vulnerability? Why did I let the abstract and the "urgent" so exhaust me, destroying the concrete and immediate good before me? I should have loved this dear man with the purity and passion of Jesus. Why did I listen to the loud and various voices of the world, rather than the still, small voice of the Holy Spirit?

Had I known Henri, better still, had I really known Jesus, I might have stopped, listened, and loved this man, and other actual neighbors and friends, with abandon. I would have, should have, could have. For, as C. S. Lewis reminds us in *The Weight of Glory*, nations and ideologies and theology will vanish, but not people. "There are no mere mortals. The glory of your neighbor, your wife, your brother, your child, a stranger, is second only to the glory of God."

If I had seen what Henri saw, I would have loved. I would have loved. I would have loved. I might have seen through my own pride and misplaced idea that God needed me to care for many to see instead the gift of love from one man right beside me. With Henri's wisdom, I might have stopped loving mankind in the abstract and started loving one man in particular. I might have looked each day and really seen his eyes, his heart. I might have better anticipated his needs. I might have attended consistently with wonder and adoration to the miracle of that exquisite life dreamed up so sweetly by the Trinity before time itself. I might have cared more about his life than my own and learned how God unites two lives and callings into one. We might have borne our own children as well as caring for the college-aged children of others: students trying to survive the anesthetic of godlessness in the air of secular universities.

I might have followed my heart of hearts.

But what happened instead? While I was imagining that I was "doing God's will," I lost this one I held most dear, and he eventually married a dear mutual friend who listened and waited better than I.

I now live with the knowledge that I failed at what matters most to me: I failed to love. Ironically, the year *Christianity Today* listed me as one of America's fifty young "up and coming" evangelical leaders was a year I failed to love.

At times I am angry with God for letting me fail. At times I am angry at this friend for leaving before I finished my commitments to others and before my new life emerged out of prayer and worship. More often I am angry at myself for my slowness of heart, lack of discipline and foresight, and foolishness to speak of truth without allowing the Person "full of grace and truth" to fully live in me as his temple. The Word became flesh and dwelled among us. How did I turn him back into words again?

I did not make enough time to see what Henri saw. Simply, I did not make enough time for Jesus. Neglecting a relationship with

Christ cost me a relationship with my friend as well—a cost that often feels unbearable given the vividness of this golden love, of a thousand tender memories, of my insatiable desire to reclaim and redeem.

Henri's vulnerability had offended me and yet now frees me to speak honestly (and perhaps foolishly) as well. I imagine that this lament will embarrass me in years to come, but if one reader chooses to love one person because of it, I am guessing that the reward will be worth the cost.

These memories raise for me some timeless questions: To which projects are we called in this life, and do they draw us to or away from the heart of Jesus? How can we really see and hear God and each other above the enemy's voices? How can we excel at expressing our faith through love? How can we artfully and sacrificially love when given the privilege? What could possibly be more important?

Jesus says that the purpose of our lives, in this order, is to love and adore God and one another with our whole being. Nothing can fulfill our whole selves except faith expressing itself concretely through love (Gal. 5:6). Why then does anyone, particularly a believer, compromise one's opportunity to live in such beauty?

My community of friends had been alive for one another. What happens when disappointment threatens to sever the future of friendships and leave only poems, photographs, and memories— mere watercolor sketches of our special moments. Skiing and hiking in the Adirondack, White, and Rocky Mountains. Joining in hay rides and barn dances. Singing. Climbing high above breaching whales off the coast of Maui. Watching the sunrise on the cratered lava summit of Haleakala. Enduring through graduate school together. Feeding the homeless and other friends with the bread we kneaded. Working for years with a million words on *Finding God at Harvard*. Making an elegant dining table upon which we may not eat. Sewing wedding quilts under which we shall not sleep. Kayaking by fire and moonlight on Winnipausakee. Camping on Mount Washington and above Yosemite in squalls and snow and lightning. Experiencing the magic of the Cape with its dunes and winds and pines. . . . A thousand quiet kindnesses make every time and place shared a diamond in the mountain of my memory.

My stepmother once said that aging is a series of losses. It must be more. How do we live without the ones we love? The wing and the wheel have carried some away; some have gone to heaven. Will we be together again? Will truth and mercy kiss at last, like long lost friends? Until that Day, is there a place where these friends, these memories, are safely hid as pearls of greatest price? Is it, O Lord, in your mindful heart? Is it, Lord, at the foot of the cross?

And Lord, for what world did you design my heart? Surely not this one. Either this world, or my heart, or both, have fallen from your original design. Some say that loss of love is like the loss of a limb. You must relearn to function. For me, loss of friendship can feel more like the loss of a vital organ: a heart perhaps, or a brain or lungs. To live through such loss is to relearn to feel, to move, to think, and to breathe.

I live near the ocean now, in the woods north of Boston. For months, the beauty of the sea was too bittersweet to take in. Beauty can be hard to bear alone—it is amplified in the sharing.

I longed to wind back the clock and to love this man I could have better loved. The saying turns out to be correct: "Hell is knowing truth too late." And hell has a voice which reminds and accuses. It begins with the doubt-inducing question of the serpent, "Has God truly said. . . ?" This voice is loud and guttural and relentless. It barks through darkness and light. It demands despair, preaching that this life is all there is and that the good life lies behind me. It says, "Your love is too late, Kelly. There will never be another chance to love." The voice of hell tells me that even Jesus has left me. Its goal is to reduce my faith and promote despair. This voice drowns me, desiring my death.

But there is another voice which calls out, "Storm, be still." It is tender and earnest, whispering to me. "I set before you life and death; choose life. I make all things new; enter this newness with me. The cross must come before the crown. Life is before you." This voice is my lifeboat, and I must do everything possible to climb inside it. In this voice, I find answers to difficult questions: How can I forgive myself and others? How wide is God's mercy? Is Jesus bigger than my mistakes? Can his will for my life include tragedy? Might I find joy once again?

The struggle winded me, and I began to read from Henri Nouwen.

Henri reminds me to breathe. His books tell me that joy and sorrow are the parents of spiritual growth. He says to not be destroyed by despair, but to trust that a good God has allowed this to happen and is not surprised by what has happened. Henri reminds me that the God who created the galaxies is bigger than the mistakes of his children—bigger than what I have done and what I have left undone, bigger than my losses and sorrows and dreams.

During the times when life seems dark and God's hand invisible, Christians must once again face their decision to trust the character of God. Even Jesus had to make this choice.

Nouwen suggests that God's sovereign goodness has allowed something to happen which, painful as it may be, holds a promise. Jesus, wrote Nouwen in *Bread for the Journey*, invites us to embrace our brokenness as he embraced the cross, and to live it as part of our mission. He asks us not to reject our brokenness as a curse from God that reminds us of our sinfulness, but to accept it as God's blessing for our purification and sanctification. Thus, our brokenness can become a gateway to new life.

Henri reminds me to pray with a listening heart. "Our ability to think is our greatest gift, but it is also the source of our greatest pain," he wrote in *Bread for the Journey*. And so he encourages me to cease the endless, internal, and corrosive loop of my thinking, and to begin to let God into a dialogue called prayer.

He encourages me to show gratitude. "The art of living," Henri wrote, "is to enjoy what we can see and not complain about what remains in the dark" even if light is shed only on our next step.

Henri says to slow down and really look at Jesus, and our families, and our friends. He encourages us to look at the stranger. He says to look and to listen, to be faithful in the little things and to live with a glad and cheerful heart. He says to be gentle with one another, and full of compassion. Henri tells us to choose joy. He reminds us that faith looks forward—and that this ability to look forward in joy is what makes us most human.

Henri felt the deep wounds of those he loved. He wrote in a journal, "You, who I expected to be there for me, you have abandoned me. How can I ever forgive you for that?" He concluded that forgiveness often seems impossible, but nothing is impossible for God. He says to pray for the grace to forgive, for forgiveness converts curses into blessings, deepens the wisdom of our hearts, and heals memories.

What are we to do? Jesus says, "Go and learn what this means: 'I desire mercy, not sacrifice'" (Matt. 9:13). He says to recognize that our anxious-driven hearts and profane culture need healing. We need conversion to a deeper way of trusting and loving.

I am learning that forgiving myself, and others, is possible only when I soak in the Father's love. Only as I receive his mercy can I offer it gracefully and naturally to others. In doing so, I am a branch abiding in the true vine, and I am choosing to love God within his perfect ecology, joining in his grand economy of grace.

Nouwen saw forgiveness as the cement of community life. "As people who have hearts that long for perfect love, we have to forgive one another for not being able to give or receive that perfect love in our everyday lives. Our many needs constantly interfere with our desire to be there for the other unconditionally. What needs to be forgiven?" he asks. "We need to forgive each other for not being God."

Nouwen speaks of the joy of sharing our humanity with others in confession and prayer, laughter and tears, forgiveness and reconciliation. The joy of Jesus is that God is with us, present tense, as things are. He is alive in those who love him.

For Henri the question is not "How can we make community?" but "How can we develop and nurture giving hearts?" How can we rejoice for others instead of mourning for ourselves?

Henri told his soul to hope, just as the psalmist wrote, "Why are you downcast, O my soul?... Put your hope in God" (Ps. 42:5). The person of hope lives in the moment with the faith that all of life is in good hands. Abraham, Moses, Ruth, Mary, and Jesus all lived with a promise in their hearts that guided them towards the future without the need to know exactly what it would look like. They had the wisdom to let go and to trust their Abba, Father.

The choice between hell and heaven seems to be the choice of which voice to follow. One voice calls forth the angst of Martha, the other calls forth the trust and stillness of her sister Mary. One points to past failure, the other to future grace.

Henri reminds us that we are chosen by God, that we are blessed. When we can hear this good voice, trust in it, and remember it, especially during dark times, we can live our lives as God's blessed children and find the strength to overcome; and then we can go on to share the love of God with others. And so it turns out that real life, life in the Kingdom of God, lies endlessly before us. "How great is the love the Father has lavished upon us, that we should be called children of God" (1 John 3:1). Why might God delight so much in the heart of children? Why might he care so greatly as to adopt and bear each of us as his own child? How can he make all things, and each life, new?

G. K. Chesterton thrilled to say that God himself is the youngest person in the universe. He is fully alive and full of potential, yet never bored with the repetition of daily faithfulness. He is always vital and brand new. That is why he can love us so faithfully.

It is this eternal newness which he wants to impart to us. Time is God's creation. It is small to his greatness. He is neither bound to time nor surprised by its passing. Shallow men, it is said, spend much time on the past while fools spend much time imagining the future. Wise men live in the present, trusting that the world is born again each morning. Henri knew this. He grew free, and he grew young.

I am learning that what matters is to choose life now, to refer quietly in my heart not to the Great I WAS, but, the Great I AM. This is faith, and it pleases God. I can die into this faith, or out of it. Christ in me is to live, and to live in this present moment in the light I am given. I am to trust that God's will is not thwarted by my slowness of heart and smallness of brain, but that his will for my life is organic, full of mysterious chemistry and deep magic, and responsive to my will to love him. C. S. Lewis tells us of an imaginary land called Narnia where "it is always winter and never Christmas." But Christmas has come! What a profound symbol it is that we celebrate God's birth into the world during the stone-cold, dead of winter.

For our salvation, the true Lord of Eden took the thorns of our rebellion, twisted them into a crown, and plunged it into his skull so we could return to the Garden and the Tree of Life. This King comes to woo us. "He comes to make his glory known far as the curse is found." He welcomes apprentices in his Kingdom who allow out-rageous things to be done in their hearts, such as the choice to bless and pray and rejoice with those who have so wounded us. The king of Narnia, representing Christ, is a lion who "is not safe, but is good." His presence inspired the horse, Hwin, to say, "You are so beautiful. I would rather be eaten by You than fed by any one else." Can we say the same to our King?

"High King of heaven my treasure Thou art," the hymn goes. This treasure, this King, offers to live within us. His Kingdom demands that we forgive ourselves, our neighbors, and the King him-self rather than rail at him in our ignorance and hurt. His rule fills us daily with joy, peace, love, and hope. I still wonder how this King, and Kingdom, will live more fully within me.

When I come to accept my own story, full of both treasure and loss, and then open the Scriptures, I find a vast and epic story of redemption to which I belong. I have learned that my vantage point is as limited as if I were looking at the starry night sky through a plas-tic straw. My comfort is that Jesus Christ is risen and alive and com-ing again in glory. This is our real story. The real story, which our Father will one day tell us himself, is not a story of disappointment but of appointment, not one of scarcity and loss but of abundance and gain, not of defeat but of victory. Today we have the choice to live today in the right story.

In the ivory tower of Harvard (where people rarely used "the J word"), Henri grew tired of mere words about theology, longing instead for Jesus himself. Henri understood that Mary, the mother of Jesus, so loved the Word of God that he chose to become flesh in her. She was a faithful hospice to God's Word. She was a crib. We too are given this same invitation to show God's hospitality and to gain holiness.

In his final days, Nouwen kept a journal called *Sabbatical Journey*. In it, he reveals as much longing as fulfillment. I sense in this longing something of the secret of Henri's greatness: in a way, he died before he died. In this life, he died to any confidence in his own vitality and sufficiency in order to live in the indestructible life of Jesus. Because he hid his life in Jesus and in the hope of the glory yet to be revealed, death did not swallow him. He remains in Christ, forever.

So when we grieve, and each of us will, we can grieve as Henri Nouwen did, with hope in a Child—the youngest person in the universe—who allows us to say "good grief."

"Heart of our own hearts, whatever befalls, still be our vision, O Ruler of all."

Nine

The Courage to Continue

by
Bob Buford

Dear Chris:
. . . As you know, this is not an easy time for me. I am living presently in Winnipeg in a community called Homes for Growth where I hope to recover my physical and emotional health. It is a time of solitude and prayer. . . .

Henri Nouwen, February 18, 1988

Bob Buford

Bob Buford of Dallas is president of a successful cable television company and the founder of Leadership Network, a support service to leaders of large churches. He is the author of *Halftime* and *Game Plan*, books that ask the readers to consider what significance they may add to the world in the second half of their lives.

HENRI Nouwen was a remarkable man. He seemed to incorporate into himself the many paradoxes of the spiritual world, being, at the same time, a wonderfully complex human being and one of the most guileless people I've ever known. He was a brilliant, sophisticated man who excelled at Harvard and Yale—places as competitive and worldly wise as any on earth—and yet, he eagerly sought to serve others humbly and simply. Henri had a marvelous intellect and a thoughtful, transparent spirit.

In his relationships, he could be an objective observer of others while at the same time valuing engagement with them. As one of the finest writers on the subject of solitude, he nevertheless chose deep engagement with mentally challenged individuals, helping them, caring for them, feeding and dressing them, praying with them, being in their presence constantly.

Most people who read Henri's work find, to their astonishment, that they connect with him immediately. They feel as if they know him, as if they can see his soul. He had the gift of allowing you to see his confusion, anguish, pain, and uncertainty as well as his spiritual harmony, deep sense of connectedness, and well-being. Somehow, it all fit together. Because he was so human—so genuine and transparent—Henri was paradoxically able, ultimately, to touch in each of us a resonant chord—a connection with the transcendent. As a humble man, he had the wonderful ability to make Christ visible.

As a child, I was given the gift of faith, so I never really struggled with questions of belief. God was real to me. Christ was real, and the struggles that many people have with their faith were never mine. But with my child-like faith came the overriding questions: What do I do with what I believe? How do I believe with integrity? How should I behave?

In answering those questions, I recognized two goals in my life— even though they seemed to be competing loyalties at the time. My first ambition was to make my mark in the world of business. Then I wanted to serve God. Through my early forties, I focused mostly on making my mark, which, in my case, meant operating a business, earning money, and feeling a great sense of accomplishment.

Henri too, I think, felt those competing loyalties. The first half of his life was dedicated to having a substantive academic career, to being taken seriously at the finest universities in the world.

But then, for both of us, came the moment I call "half-time"— that point in life when a person decides to make a transition from success to significance. I detected that in Henri when he left the academic community to begin his relationship with L'Arche. He chose to move toward an intimacy with God, toward making a difference in just a few people's lives—and away from the need to "make his mark" in the world. Still, in the three times I met Henri, never did I sense that he was a monastic or inaccessible or off in another world. As he grew more intimate with God, he also seemed to grow more intimate with everyone he encountered.

One good friend of mine, who has attended both the Harvard Business School and Boston University, where she worked with renowned thinker Peter Berger, now attends Harvard Divinity School. There, she has just completed research on the relationship between the clergy and the laity, and in her study she discovered that there is almost no relationship between today's clergy and laity, that they live in two separate worlds that barely touch except at ceremonial services on the weekends. In my experience, Henri was an exception to this rule. He cut through barriers and extended himself in significant ways to the people he knew.

He had not one shred of arrogance in him—not one. To have sold as many books as he sold, to be as much in demand as he was, and to accomplish as much as he did, many would have thought him the true inheritor of Thomas Merton's legacy as a spiritual writer. But he approached me, as he approached everyone he met, as if I were the most interesting person he'd ever met.

My wife, Linda, and I had dinner with Henri one evening in Fort Worth, Texas, and we were surprised that he seemed so concerned about what was going on in our lives. We were on his agenda; he was thinking about us.

When I first read Henri's work, something clicked in my mind. I knew immediately, even before meeting him, that I would grow to admire him. It was not his knowledge that drew me to him, nor his spiritual authority. It is just the power of his being. Few people have it: Mother Teresa had it for sure. Saint Francis surely had it. Henri was able to teach the Gospel just by being.

I find it interesting to watch the baby boomers, especially to see the struggles of the recovering materialists of that generation. The leading edge of the boomers is fifty-one years old. At that half-time in their lives, they begin to live a whole second adulthood that people in previous generations never had. In 1900, life expectancy was fifty years old. Now, many of us can expect twenty or thirty more years of reasonably good health, more affluence than any generation has ever had before. How will we use that extra time and money? Reading Henri's books would be a good place to start in answering that question.

One of Henri's great victories was over his own self-consciousness. When he was in pain, he was able to get beyond the inhibitions that most of us feel. Henri, because of his humility and sense of service for others, was able to articulate his emotions, to put them into writing, so that they might be useful to others. But he was never self-indulgent. He was never simply performing therapy on himself just to feel better or have a "cathartic experience." He did it for his readers. He wrote about his owns sufferings as a way of giving to others.

It was, perhaps, on the subject of suffering that Henri was most eloquent. When my wife, Linda, and I lost our only son in 1987 at age twenty-four, we learned a great lesson about suffering. For me, the experience broke through my self-sufficiency. It threw me to my knees to pray as I've never prayed before. And though I could not bring my son back, God bountifully answered my prayers. I began to keep a journal of those answered prayers for a while, and in three months' time, I wrote down 165 things that I thought were graces that God had given me to comfort me in that agonizing period. Not the least of those graces was one that I knew Henri would understand especially: I became more accessible to other people. I allowed them to minister to me.

Like most of us, I had spent so much time trying to appear capable and in control, but all we achieve by such efforts is that we hold people at arm's length. Then, suddenly, after my son's death, I became the kind of person I least expected to be: a huggable person. A needy person.

I recall that when a humble older employee in the custodial department of my company heard about my son's death, she came to me, put her arms around me, and just hugged me. She wept and said incomprehensible things over my shoulder, but somehow, I understood everything. It is in those moments that God's grace does indeed become real to us, and we realize that surrender to that grace is one of life's most important events.

Generally, when we are self-sufficient, we render ourselves inaccessible to others and to God as well. But suffering opens us up, teaches us our dependence, and for me, Henri opened that channel. In his books he expressed in words, more powerfully than I ever could, the fact that hope does exist, that grace is real, and that God will never abandon us.

One of Henri's most interesting insights came that night we had dinner with him in Fort Worth. I had explained to him the thesis of my book *Half Time*, which is about mid-life not as a crisis but as an opportunity. In that book I explain my idea that most of us pass from a concern for success to a need for significance. But Henri suggested that I'd missed two other stages. First, there is the struggle stage, when a person wants to be successful but isn't. This might create enough of a crisis to cause a person to give up the struggle to succeed. But there is also another necessary stage, which Henri called "surrender." Without surrender, a person would be too angry to give up all the things he or she must give up before seeking true significance. It was clear to me at that moment that Henri was a person who was always ready to surrender everything if necessary.

Now, like my son, Henri is gone. Part of Henri's legacy is that we can experience joy even in the midst of our suffering. He embodied that kind of joy. Death was okay for him. He was always ready to surrender. He didn't cling to life greedily, and his life was more vibrant because of it.

But even now I think of Henri as a guide, as someone who has gone before me to explore the uncharted territory. I have a sense that he is with my son Ross right now, and that they like one another, that they are friends. I am glad that he and Ross both have that level of peace and joy that, in many ways, I long for as well. I have a sense that each of them broke free from the pull of gravity. They have found surrender.

For the time being, the rest of us are, like Dante, lost in the dark woods of life. If you need a guide, however, I recommend the books of Henri Nouwen. He is an expert guide through this jungle.

Three days after I heard the news of Henri's death, a remarkable thing happened. I received a package. From Henri. From L'Arche. I thought, well this must be a book he's working on that his publisher sent. I opened the package, and there, inside the front cover of one of Henri's newest books, was an inscription—from Henri. The book has Henri's picture on the back—a really wonderful picture. In that face, I could see all his complexities, all the paradoxes he embodied, all the suffering he had experienced. Receiving that book and seeing that picture made me feel as if he were still alive. To me he is. For me and for countless other readers, Henri isn't gone. He's simply walking on ahead.

Ten

With an Open Heart, the Journey Is Simpler

by

Ed Wojcicki

Dear Chris:
. . . Thanks for being such a good friend. . . .
                                    Henri Nouwen, January 23, 1989

Ed Wojcicki

Ed Wojcicki is a journalist who has logged more than two decades as a reporter, editor, and freelance writer. He worked for several daily newspapers in Missouri and Illinois and also worked full time for the Catholic press for seven years (1985–92). Since 1992 he has been publisher of *Illinois Issues*, a monthly magazine that focuses on government, politics, and life in Illinois, and is published by the University of Illinois at Springfield.

A graduate of the University of Missouri School of Journalism, Mr. Wojcicki is the author of the book *A Crisis of Hope in the Modern World*. His wife, Sally, is the co-owner of two businesses in Springfield, Illinois, and they have two children, Sara and Luke.

I ALWAYS admired the special bond between my wife, Sally, and our next-door neighbor. Jack was a widower. Nearly seventy, he lived alone and had a zest for life, going to his own accounting office every day, going bowling, and staying involved in local politics.

From the time we moved next to him, he always treated us warmly. "Ahoy!" Jack, a Navy veteran, would shout through the yard whenever he would drive up and see us anywhere outside. We chatted with him frequently, usually on the spur of the moment when we would cross paths outside.

Each year Sally would plant flowers in Jack's yard, near his front porch and along his driveway, and she would water them faithfully every day in the spring and summer. She found great satisfaction in transforming unattended or overgrown areas into a place of natural beauty, and Jack would periodically comment how beautiful his yard looked, thanks to Sally.

Jack loved to talk and to offer lengthy theories about current economic and political events; so much so, in fact, that sometimes when I saw him driving up I would hurry inside to avoid any conversation beyond "Ahoy!"

Now that Jack is dead, I feel ashamed of what I occasionally did. But I see my calculated avoidance of Jack as one little pixel in a much bigger picture. This much I know: Little things irritate me. They annoy me. Little things like interruptions or phone calls from other people when I'm in the middle of something. I catch myself feeling impatient with whomever interrupts, and I react on the inside with aggravation. When this squirms out of me toward others as abruptness or indifference or annoyance, I know in an instant I don't really mean it, but damage has been done. I am not proud of the fact that when I search my soul, I consider too many little things as intrusions on my life. Maybe nobody notices. Or maybe only those closest to me know it, because around them I have been guilty of my greatest failures to be responsive and present.

Far too often, my mind drifts away, especially with little things. I start thinking about what I might be doing next, or what else I could be doing. Then I get anxious about whatever is next, and this pattern deprives me of many joys of the moment. The problem for me is more pronounced in personal relationships and social settings than in professional relationships at work, where I understand how to play a role. I understand that life in the present is the most precious time of all, but I constantly grapple with trying to live as though that's true.

The biggest reason I appreciate Henri Nouwen's writing is that he often admitted how great the battle is to overcome one's own weaknesses. By doing so in such a public way, he gently gave me permission to live with my own struggles and failures, while never allowing me to accept that I cannot change.

I also love Nouwen's work because he unashamedly used the word *broken* to describe himself—and by inference, me. Nouwen teaches that in the recognition of our weaknesses—our brokenness—liberation begins. This liberation leads us to hope: to choosing hope over cynicism, compassion over competition, hospitality over hostility.

For me, liberation begins when I recognize my broken condition and choose to respond to interruptions with concern and attentiveness rather than irritation. Nouwen tenaciously trumpeted the trait I need to adopt to change my reactions. He called it hospitality. At first I thought hospitality meant doing certain tasks or embracing a certain lifestyle. But Nouwen's concept means much more than being cordial or playing the role of polite host or hostess in social settings. His kind of hospitality is more profound: It is an attitude of the heart that is always alert and alive in the present moment. The hospitable heart spontaneously offers a safe place for other people to share their concerns and feel respected, and at the same time, it reaches out to others. The hospitable heart paints the existing moment with so many colorful pixels that even mundane tasks take on new meaning.

Martin Luther King Jr. used to say that street sweepers should sweep streets with the same pride that Michelangelo painted. Everyday duties feel so different when adorned with bright colors and splashes of light! Such tasks are no longer a bother or an obligation, but opportunities for connecting with others and being of service to them—like Sally's affection for nurturing Jack's flowers every year to make sure his yard looked nice.

My life as a journalist, husband, and father has been a mixture of growing professionally, earning a living, and making a contribution to a healthy family and community. Outside observers would probably call me successful, but as I go about my business year after year, I have never been too distant from my inner world's nagging disillusionment with my own inconsistencies.

In addition to my day job in university publishing, I try to devote part of my mornings and weekends to writing, sometimes just for myself and other times for publication. Writing is that important to me, but other daily living tasks usually get in the way, like finishing up dishes from the night before, ironing my clothes for the day, skimming two daily newspapers, and taking care of our dog's morning needs.

One weekend morning after I did a little writing, the rest of the family awoke, and I opted to stop to take my daughter, Sara, to her summer job at a department store. She drives, but if I wanted a car any time during that day, I needed to give her a ride to work. On the way out of the house, I noticed that the hardware holding the wooden screen door to the house had pulled away. Oh, well, I thought, I'll just fix the door later and get it over with. So I took Sara to work and then stopped by the hardware store. I don't know what got into me, but I bought not only the hardware to fix the door but some shelving that I've been thinking about installing in an upstairs closet for about ten years. I drove home, leaned the shelving aside and spent a couple of hours fixing the front door. Then I remembered Sara mentioning along the drive to work that she had forgotten to take the lunch that she had asked me to make for her. So after fixing the door I chose to make another trip to the department store where Sara works. I arrived just in time for her break, and she quietly expressed gratitude and accepted the lunch.

By the time I got home again, the afternoon was more than half over, and after washing the dishes left in the sink and watching a couple of innings of the Cubs-Cardinals baseball game on WGN (thanks to cable), well, not much time was left for writing. Oh, well. Another day of feeling less productive than I wanted to be. The point is that I still have much to learn about my own responses to the ordinary activities that fill my days.

I love opportunities that bond me more closely with my children. Taking my daughter to work gives me fifteen minutes for one-on-one chatting, when I always learn something new about what she thinks. How wonderful, but I often feel cheated of "my time" when other little annoyances, like a broken front door, pop up. I would be better off just accepting these as part of the rhythm of life, because fretting about them does nothing more than sap precious energy from my day.

"I am impatient, restless, full of preoccupations, and easily suspicious," Nouwen wrote in *The Genesee Diary*. During his seven months at a Trappist Monastery in New York state, he found it boring to do routine tasks such as packing bread, washing raisins, pressing sheets, and collecting stones from a creek, hours at a time. He bluntly admitted he did not enjoy such work, but he noticed that the older monks "really enjoyed their work and did not feel as I do." The lesson for him was profound. He learned from his discomfort with routine tasks how alienated and disconnected he was from his immediate world.

For Nouwen boredom emanated from washing raisins and collecting stones. For me over the years, there have been many hours of boredom in folding laundry, cleaning the house, and handling inevitable and always inconvenient household repairs. To the extent that I find such tasks a nuisance rather than projects to be done out of love for others, I get resentful or angry that I am not spending those moments doing something more important, though I am hard pressed to define exactly what I mean by "something more important." Just "something else," I guess. Even worse, I admit with some amusement, sometimes I waste even more time fretting about doing the unwanted tasks before getting to them, and then I get more frustrated about whittling away my days.

Nouwen devoted an entire section of his book *Reaching Out* to becoming a hospitable rather than a hostile person. He noted in that 1975 book that "being busy" has become a status symbol that unfortunately prevents people from creating loving space for others in their lives.

Henri wrote a lot about creating an "empty space" in your heart—like a guest room in your house—so there is room for others to feel welcome. The problem is, when I nearly drown in my own schedules and agenda, I leave no room for others and no time for hospitality. So I face a lifelong task of conversion in learning to understand that the little things in relationships with others are always a gift and an opportunity. I have discovered that when I allow my heart to contain too much resentment, busyness and anxiety, especially anxiety about getting to my next appointment or wishing I were doing something else, I leave no room in my heart for others. I raise a wall around me, and others probably wonder why they can't come in. I imagine some of them go away sadly, tired of encountering a closed heart.

A hospitable heart kicks out all preoccupations. Usually when I get home from work, my wife and I mingle in the kitchen as she prepares dinner.

Sally owns and runs two small businesses, and she often tells me stories about something that happened to her that day. Most days I enjoy these stories, and we talk about the ups and downs of the workaday world. I have learned much about living from her experiences as an entrepreneur and her ability to make connections with people throughout the day. Our after-work conversations go best when we listen well and share experiences, but sometimes when she asks me what I think, I realize I was thinking about something else, or I'm tired from my own travails, or in my head I'm preparing a comment that may or may not be a direct response to what she's talking about. I regret it each time it happens. An absence of presence from me—such inhospitality—deprives her of having an important human connection, and it robs me of an opportunity for give-and-take that could enrich our relationship. And sometimes at work, someone will begin to tell me about something that happened to him or her, and too soon my mind drifts ahead to what I'll be doing when the conversation is over. I don't realize I'm doing this until the person finishes the story and I am able to mutter only generic words of consolation or understanding because I was only half-listening.

The paradox is that I know how to be a good listener with my wife, my children, and my coworkers, and often I am. A friend who was going through a divorce dropped by our office one day, and I made a point to ask him to sit for a minute, only so I could ask him how things were going. Not very well, he told me, and the story got long. So I calmly listened to his stories and empathized with him. There was nothing else I could do, but it was the best thing to do. I solved nothing, but the bond of understanding between this man and me during that time made both of us feel better. At that moment I simply opened my heart. He felt welcome, and he entered.

Being open and prepared for interruptions comes naturally to a hospitable person. I began to appreciate Nouwen's passion for such openness on the very first page of the first of his books that I read. During my college years, someone introduced me to *With Open Hands*. On the first page he tells the story of someone who has a clenched fist. Inside her fist is a coin she does not want to give up, fearing that if she gave up that last possession, "she would have nothing more, and be nothing more." So life is a process of opening our hands freely to accept the personal and material gifts offered by God and others.

I have never been able to forget that image of living with a clenched fist. I have spent my entire adult life with closed or partially closed fists, stubbornly holding on to one thing or another. Sometimes it's been ambition, other times a bullheaded belief that I was right when I was really wrong about something, and other times a little irritation with others. Other times I have enjoyed the rewards of opening my fist in friendship and other good relationships, but I have found Henri's warning to be true that another closed fist always lurks behind the first one, clinging to something else.

The process of opening up never ends. But it is essential for a hospitable person.

In addition to hospitality, Henri was also fascinated—and troubled—by the lure of power, personal power. So am I. When I decided to become a journalist, I often dreamed of being successful and powerful. I enrolled at the highly acclaimed University of Missouri School of Journalism, and friends soon began asking only half-jokingly when I would land at the *New York Times*. I am sure I surprised many of them when I took my first job at a very small daily newspaper, the *Monmouth Daily Review Atlas*, in a little western Illinois town two hundred miles north of Saint Louis and light-years from Chicago. This rural and unheralded region is so remote that even residents there self-deprecatingly refer to it as "Forgottonia," but it was a place to start a career, pay my dues, and find an outlet to the outside world, mostly by freelance writing.

Monmouth proved to be much more than a starting point. I met Sally, who became my wife. We also had our two children while living there, and we got our early education in mortgages, car payments, and leaky roofs.

Even there, I now realize, my mind would often drift into the future: wondering what I would be doing next; wondering at many routine moments why I couldn't be doing something else, something more fulfilling, in a more exciting place. I particularly remember a favorite high school teacher from Saint Louis asking me, "What do you do in Monmouth, watch the grass grow?" Such are the stereotypes that go along with small-town living. That is unfortunate, because for all of their lack of bustle, small-town living naturally produces and embraces more community-wide caring and compassion than larger cities, where people seem busier and more anonymous.

Henri would understand the importance of watching the grass grow, of nurturing ourselves and finding space for others no matter what our circumstances are. We eventually did move: a hundred miles south to Springfield, Illinois—Lincoln's hometown and burial place. I went with my new young family and with a clenched fist or two.

As editor of the diocesan Catholic weekly newspaper in Springfield, my love of Nouwen's writing led me to write my first "open letter" to him in 1986. I used Henri's ideas to reflect on my own spirituality and share some of my confusion and spiritual struggles with my readers, just as Henri did with his. I am no Henri Nouwen, of course—just a country editor, as I sometimes call myself—but I found a kinship with Henri's struggles. I mailed him a copy of the first open letter, and he responded with a kind note, in which he invited me to stay in touch. So I did. The tradition of annual open letters lasted six years, until I left that job. Each year Henri would respond privately with a letter of his own, and we exchanged other letters as well, even after I moved to another job in Springfield as publisher of a magazine about Illinois government and politics.

All along, Henri inspired me with candid reflections about his spiritual struggles. One year he responded to my open letter by thanking me for reminding him what he had written: "My own writing sometimes expresses better where I want to be spiritually than where I am," he admitted. "So it is very good to be confronted by my own words. It is humbling, but also hopeful." That is another of Henri's comments that is seared into me, just like the image of the clenched fist, for I often find myself confronted by my own words as well—knowing what to do, but never quite living up to my own expectations.

Enough. Enough beating up on myself. I feel so tempted to keep emphasizing my shortcomings, as if I want to shout for all to hear that I have faults and problems and issues to deal with. I want to beat to death the point that life is a struggle, lest I seem too syrupy or soft about the difficulties of living a Christian life in a secular culture that publicly adulates material and professional successes, but I don't want to be so hard on myself—which I sometimes am—that I don't leave myself enough space to see my goodness as well as my weaknesses.

Henri warned us not to engage in negative "spiritual exhibitionism." In *The Wounded Healer*, he said it's wrong to focus too much on our flaws. "Open wounds stink and do not heal," he wrote. So I need to move on, trying to discover what life has to offer, how I can soothe my struggles and salve my weaknesses. This is precisely where Henri has been so helpful. For him, learning to live with weaknesses and brokenness and loneliness was important, but not nearly as important as learning to transcend imperfections by choosing hope and being connected to others.

Nouwen became a persistent prophet of hope and hospitality. While writing considerably about feeling wounded, he adamantly avoided a temptation to romanticize weaknesses, and he never defended wallowing in a state of self-declared victimization. He taught about one of the great paradoxes of life: that only through inevitable woundedness and suffering and pain can we emerge to be connected to others.

Toward the end of 1988, one of the hardest years of his life, Henri wrote me:

> Never have I felt so strongly how great pain and anguish can lead to new life, new hope, new courage. On one level I feel more fragile than ever; on another level I feel stronger than ever because of God's so tangible presence in my life. So I feel very close to the words of St. Paul: in weakness there is strength.

Henri helped me understand that I can find meaning in my life because of—not in spite of—the weaknesses I endure with some loneliness every day. Henri taught that we can and should choose hope in the midst of a chaotic, corrupt, and very imperfect world.

More than twenty years since I first saw it, I still admire a photograph of a child in *With Open Hands*. Taken by Theo Robert, the black-and-white picture shows the child looking slightly upward, over the camera, with wide-open eyes that are at once asking questions, reaching out and expressing love. Most remarkable about this child is that his right arm is extended outward in front of him. He is reaching out in great anticipation to someone or something, palm upward, and fingers spread apart. This child is far removed from having a clenched fist. He has created a space for the other to enter into his world, and he does so freely and without conditions. I want to be that hopeful person wherever I go.

Knowing that I'll never quite get there is what makes hope the most meaningful virtue for me. Because of my own shortcomings and the human imperfection all around me, it is easy to slip into cynicism, finger-pointing, and frustration. The great temptation is to drop out, to stop trying, to be less than what I'm called to be because of the great tension involved in never getting there. With hope in the heart, however, life takes on a new meaning. Hope gives life meaning. How important hope becomes in our places of work, where our culture preaches the importance of success and power.

"Unfortunately," Henri wrote in *Adam*, a book not published until after his death, "there is a very loud, consistent, and powerful message coming to us from our world that leads us to believe that we must prove our belovedness by how we look, by what we have, and by what we can accomplish." This was essentially the same message Henri warned about years earlier in his book *In the Name of Jesus*. He described there how the devil tempted Jesus in three ways: to be spectacular, to be powerful, and to be relevant, and Jesus rejected all three. Henri helped me understand how I face the same three temptations. The big temptation is to make success as defined by our culture a priority. Giving in to this temptation would require me to protect all of my plans, schedules, and schemes in a clenched fist that would prevent me from creating open spaces for others.

My dream of fame and power never quite goes away. But what if it never happens? What if my life takes several turns for the worse, as it did with Job? What then? Enter hope, says Henri. Hope teaches that my life has meaning and purpose not because of what happens with my career or money or possessions, but because of a simple yet profound promise from God always to be in relationship with me. My response, then, to this promise becomes a hopeful longing for a hospitable connection with others and with God.

The reality is that I am an imperfect husband, imperfect father, and an imperfect boss. I still expend too much energy on dashed desires, anxiety, and resentment.

Another reality is that I have many choices. I am always choosing, hour by hour. As Henri wrote in the foreword to my book, *A Crisis of Hope in the Modern World*, "Our great temptation remains to live as though we don't have a choice and to behave like pitiful victims of circumstances over which we have no control. The great spiritual challenge is to claim our inner freedom and to choose life, joy, peace and hope."

For this challenge to be real, it has to become more than a platitude. Choose! That is the beginning of the message. Choose hope! That is the second part. Choose to celebrate opportunities rather than resent problems and interruptions. When it becomes necessary to fix the front door, do it. Choose to celebrate the opportunity rather than resent the fact that it has to be done. When it comes time to write a report to satisfy the bureaucracy at the office, do it and do a great job with it rather than moan about what a time waster it is. And when it comes time to celebrate something really positive, like a child graduating from high school, take it on as a continuous series of events and moments in which to rejoice, rather than a to-do list to take care of. Such an attitude opens the heart to unforeseen possibilities in connecting to other people.

I frequently travel to Chicago on business. One time I needed a quick overnight stay, but due to a major convention in the city, few hotel rooms were available. The only one I could find was priced at $320 a night at the Hyatt Regency. That's far more than my university can afford. I was stuck. So I called a friend with some connections and asked if he could help me. Why sure, he said instantly, and he found a nice place for me right along the Magnificent Mile downtown. I tell this story not because he had the connection to get me a place to stay, but to emphasize the reason I called him. I called him because I knew he has a generous and hospitable heart. I called because I knew he would say, "Why sure!" and he would do his best to help me. Like many men (I know this is sexist) I am often reluctant to ask for help from others, but I knew something about my friend's heart. It's a heart that always has space for me and that always has a way of responding joyfully, as if he were desiring an interruption from me. I called him because I knew I would feel acceptance, regardless of whether he could get me a room. I like to observe this friend and learn from him how satisfying it must feel to have a heart like that, to be so hospitable by nature.

Remember my neighbor Jack? He died suddenly at the age of seventy, just before the end of winter. Soon enough spring arrived, plants blossomed and his grass began to grow. Higher and higher the grass grew. (What do I do in Springfield, watch the grass grow?) So one day before dinner, I went to my garage, got out my lawnmower and cut Jack's yard. A week later, I mowed his grass again. Nobody asked me to. Nobody thanked me for it. I just felt in my heart I wanted to do it for Jack. As I cut rows back and forth in his yard, I kept glancing up at his house. I thought of how I had loved Jack, though I never expressed it that way to him, and I missed him. Though my fingers were gripping the mower's handle, my hands were not tightly fisted. They were open to service, to love, to connecting. I had a new space in my heart for Jack after all! All sense of time and duty and doing something more important somewhere else vanished as I mowed his yard. Just like the monks who collect stones for hours and appreciate the cadence of that type of labor.

Ahoy.

Eleven

Journey's End, Journey's Beginning

Dear Chris:

. . . . I sense from how you write that it is easier for you to write to a healthy person than a sick one, and that, indeed, you feel a little awkward with my being quite beaten up! Be assured, my friend, that I am in really good spirits, that I am laughing a lot, and that I feel closer to God and to my friends than ever. Although I broke five ribs and had my spleen removed, I have experienced this accident as a real grace, and as an invitation from God to slow down, to spend more time with friends, to pray more, and to trust more deeply that God truly cares for His people. I was very close to death, but didn't feel afraid. At one point, I was even a little disappointed that God hadn't called me home yet! But I know God has something left for me to do, and I am really enjoying being alive and well. . . .

Henri Nouwen, March 9, 1989

I END this book with an interview Fr. John Catoir conducted for the television program *Christopher Closeup*. Fr. John was the director of The Christophers in New York City, an organization dedicated to the notion that it is better to light one candle than curse the darkness; that one person can make a difference in this world.

I wanted to end this book with Henri's own words. It is through the word that we are still alive: the Word of God, the word of a loved one, the word of memory. And in the word there is a promise. Henri believed in that promise. In the beginning there was light, and God promised us that light in the end as well. Henri reminded me again and again that God promised to take care of us.

JOHN CATOIR: Hello. Thanks so much for joining us. Our guest today is a man of varied achievements: a writer, a lecturer, a college professor, counselor, and through all of these roles, a priest. He's authored more than twenty books on subjects ranging from intimacy and bereavement to global politics and spirituality. His most recent book is entitled *Beyond the Mirror*. So please welcome the Rev. Henri Nouwen. Henri, happy to have you with us.

HENRI NOUWEN: Well, thank you. Glad to be here.

JOHN CATOIR: You have so many hats that you wear, can you tell me a little bit about your decision to become a priest, and how you eventually chose psychology as a specialty?

HENRI NOUWEN: Well, I have hardly any memories of a time I did not want to be a priest. Since I was five years old, I saw the priesthood as something I desired, really. For a few moments, I wanted to be a captain on a boat because I liked the uniform so much. But except for that, I think I always desired to be a priest. And I remember my grandmother who had a big store. She encouraged that by giving me many things to play priest with. In those days, that was quite normal.

JOHN CATOIR: Where was this?

HENRI NOUWEN: In Holland. I was born close to Amerschroid. It's a tiny city. I lived for most of my youth close to Amsterdam in the Hague.

JOHN CATOIR: After you grew up, chose to be a priest, and were ordained, you were sent to graduate studies by your superiors. Who chose psychology, and why?

HENRI NOUWEN: Yes, it was interesting. The Bishop asked me to study theology, and I really fought that a little bit, then I said I'd really like to study psychology, and the reason was that I just wanted to know more what went on in the human heart. I didn't study psychology to become a psychologist. I studied psychology more to be able to be a better minister, to, in a way, connect the message of the Gospel more directly with the very concrete human experience of every day. I wanted to do that. I tell you, studying psychology gave me all the opportunities. I worked for a long time in the mines in Holland. I worked in a butter factory. I worked with asthmatic children. I worked in the army as a testing psychologist. I had real opportunities to get to know different people and different ways of life and to understand more about them.

JOHN CATOIR: You must have excelled in some way because you crossed the ocean and came to teach at Harvard and Yale here in the States. How did that happen?

HENRI NOUWEN: When I finished my psychological studies, I still felt a need to connect my theological, spiritual interests with my psychological knowledge. I wanted to integrate that, so I went to the Menninger Clinic in Topeka, Kansas, for a few years of sort of post-graduate work. That was an incredibly important time for me, I think the most formative time, actually, in Kansas. I received very personal attention, real supervision. People really listened to me very carefully. They were interested in what I had to do, and they gave me some confidence. I guess that's where, for the first time in my life, I started to trust my own feelings and to not be afraid of expressing them and saying yes, what I live and what I think is worth expressing. That experience there brought me connections with many people, many of them at the University of Notre Dame. And so I was invited to come to the University of Notre Dame near Chicago, in South Bend, Indiana. I taught psychology there for a few years, then I went back to Holland, but then I was invited to come to Yale and I stayed basically in the United States since that time.

JOHN CATOIR: I know you from your books, I've read your books over the years, for many years, and one of the things that stood out in my mind was that you shared yourself in your writing. In one of your books, *The Wounded Healer*, you weren't pontificating, and you weren't trying to tell people how they should live the life of perfection, you were speaking from your own wounded life.

HENRI NOUWEN: It is interesting that you say that because the book, I wrote it shortly after I definitely left Holland to come to the United States and to start teaching at

Yale, at the divinity school. I experienced a deep loneliness, an enormous, inner kind of alienation even when I left my country. Here I was in New Haven, Connecticut, I had left Holland, my family, my friends. I decided to make a life in the United States, and I experienced pain and felt a deep absence of friendship, but then I started to slowly realize that maybe the experience of loneliness and the experience of separation might not be a negative thing. It might, I thought, bring me more in touch with other people's experience of loneliness. If I would not run away from it, but feel it through all the way, it might become fruitful. Then suddenly I had this idea that loneliness which is pain, when you do not run away from it but feel it through and stand up in it and look it right in the face, that there is something there that can be a source of hope, that in the middle of the pain there is some hidden gift. I, more and more in my life, have discovered that the gifts of life are often hidden in the places that hurt most.

JOHN CATOIR: Can you tell us how you make the connection, because most of us, myself included, when we feel the discomfort of loneliness or emotional pain, the tendency is to want to run away from it and seek relief. You are saying there is a better way?

HENRI NOUWEN: Yes. I am saying that you can stand in the pain. I think one of the great challenges of life is to dare to stand in your pain, and to trust that there is something beyond that which is safe.

JOHN CATOIR: What begins to happen?

HENRI NOUWEN: What begins to happen is something like the experience that there is safety beyond the pain, that if you enter into it, it's not so frightening as you thought it was, and that underneath your loneliness, there is an experience of being held safe.

JOHN CATOIR: By whom?

HENRI NOUWEN: I don't want to right away say by God, although that is what I came to more and more. I want to say that we are held safe by life that is larger than us, by love that is stronger than fear. There is something greater. For me, that's been the courage of living, to enter into the pain and to discover underneath a love that has a personal name.

JOHN CATOIR: I wonder if it is part of God's design to bring us to Him through the pain of life? Sometimes we don't find ourselves adequate to deal with the situation and we fall back on something else, this support that you speak of.

HENRI NOUWEN: I know it for myself so much that if I experience loneliness or anguish, I distract myself. I go do something so that I don't feel it. But it is always a disappointment, and I am more lonely; I am more anguished. Then I discovered that if I just stay with it, and live with it to the fullest.

JOHN CATOIR: Accept it?

HENRI NOUWEN: Not just accept it, but taste it, chew on it. I would nearly say to myself I am lonely, yes, and let me feel it. I've discovered that there's much more strength in me than I realized and, in a way, the strength is not coming from me, but it is coming indeed from someone who holds me, who loved me long before I came into life, from someone who will love me long after I have died. It is not an intellectual thing.

JOHN CATOIR: We haven't said the word "Jesus" in this, and I wonder how you would place Jesus into this experience?

HENRI NOUWEN: Jesus for me is the center of it. Jesus for me is the one who helps me discover that God had loved me before I even was born, and will still love me after I die. The love of God is a love that is there before and after any other human being has touched me. The mystery of knowing Jesus is the mystery of knowing God who embraces me much in a wider and deeper way, more than any human being can do. It sounds quite theoretical, but I have only discovered this gradually in life through much of my own pain, and through much of my own disappointment, and through much of my own running away to other places. I guess that is why I eventually decided to go to different places in my life.

JOHN CATOIR: Following your career has been fascinating because, I would say in terms of success, you've been quite successful. Your books have been published all over the world and translated in how many languages?

HENRI NOUWEN: Ten.

JOHN CATOIR: Ten languages, and you have hundreds of thousands, perhaps millions of readers. People have resonated with your experiences through life. Most recently you survived an accident that nearly killed you. You speak about this in your book, *Beyond the Mirror*. As I read it, it brought me to a closer, deeper understanding of facing death.

HENRI NOUWEN: It all started simply: with my own impatience. I wanted to get somewhere at seven in the morning, and it was icy and slippery and I couldn't take my car, so I decided to walk. When I came to the main road, I got impatient and I wanted to hitchhike, so I stood on the road. It was a foggy morning and I got mad. I actually got mad at people who didn't stop. It doesn't make much sense but, in fact, I was mad at those people who were driving their car alone, and they had three places left and didn't stop for me. Poor me. And I said, well, why didn't you stop? Why didn't you stop? And I have an important meeting to attend.

JOHN CATOIR: And it was freezing and icy.

HENRI NOUWEN: It was freezing and icy, but people obviously were not interested. So finally I got much too close to the traffic. Maybe I just wanted to force people to stop. A little van just hit me with the mirror, the right mirror, and pushed me right up and I fell on the road and I broke many ribs. The man who hit me came to me and brought me to the emergency ward at the hospital. Then I realized that it was more than a few broken ribs, and that I was really very close to death. I am basically a nervous person. I am not at all the peaceful person. Then a surprise came, like a spiritual surprise. I suddenly realized that I might not live much longer. I had this deep, deep sense of peace, and not only that, but a deep sense that Jesus concretely appeared to me and said, "Don't be afraid. You can always come home. I've been waiting for you, and you've been waiting for me, and this is the time to come home." I had this deep sense that I was ready to go. Now, I had some difficulties in letting go, and that was very interesting. You know, my problem in dying was that I had some conflicts with some people that were not resolved, some people that I was angry with, some people who were angry with me, some people I had not forgiven, and others who had not forgiven me. A friend of mine came and

I said that if I die, please tell these people that I have forgiven them and ask them to forgive me, and when I let go of that, I felt totally ready to move right into the new place, the place that Jesus had prepared for me. I really had that experience very deep in me. It was not a facade. It was a sense of safety: okay, you're safe; you're loved. So when I was put on the table to be operated on, and I saw the nurse putting this anesthetic in me, I thought, well it's my way home. I'm ready to go. I just felt wonderful. So you can imagine when I woke up the next day, and I was back in the emergency room . . . it was somewhat of a disappointment.

Conclusion

I WOKE up early this morning and looked out my window. A single oak leaf fell from the tree, spinning like a pinwheel. Roe was still asleep beside me. Our children were sleeping in their rooms. The dog did not stir. I thought about the acorn pipe.

There was a time, many Octobers ago, when I made acorn pipes. Boys in America made acorn pipes.

I owned a miniature pocket knife. The handle was blue; a small chain hung from one end. Once long ago when the leaves turned yellow I stepped out onto the back porch of my father's house. The cold air already caused the onion grass to droop, and the ferns to shrivel. Dry day-lily stalks tipped backward. Autumn. Perhaps this was the season where I first took a backward glance at my life, seeing all that was summer, and my sister Anne swimming under my legs, and then we stood beside the ice-cream truck with quarters in our hands, and all was slipping away to winter, and we didn't know it. Perhaps this is the season where men forget the size of their bank accounts and retirement funds and begin to fish inside their pockets for a small, blue pen knife.

I ran down the porch stairs and into the garden. We had a large oak tree just inside the woods, to the left of the campfire my brother built when we were children. The stones are still there in a circle, and under the leaves and soil there are still bits of charred wood.

My brother baked apples in the fires he lit in 1958 when the smoke curled around us as I pulled my knees up to my chest. Who knows the smell of cooked apples and burning brown sugar? We liked to poke the apples with long sticks and release the steam from the center.

You cannot make acorn pipes with just any acorn. It has to be just the right color: brown, not green. It must be the right size: big. I thought once when I was a child that there existed in California acorns the size of footballs for I saw pictures of the giant redwood trees and assumed that other trees were also that large: apple trees producing apples the size of pumpkins, and pear trees heavy with pears the size of fishbowls.

There is not much to notice about a boy walking in the woods searching for an acorn. It is said that the only manmade object visible from orbit is the Great Wall of China. I do not think the astronauts noticed me in my sneakers as I stooped to my harvest; but I found my own star, my own bit of autumn in the size of the acorn that I held in my hand.

I have seen people create cars on potter's wheels, mold silver into bracelets, sketch flowers and dancers on a white canvas. I am not an artist; was never meant to be, but I felt a hint of the creative power when I opened my small knife and began to dig into the top of the acorn. A pipe holds the tobacco in the bowl. I made my acorn bowl, then bore a small hole into the side of the acorn and squeezed a small stick into my pipe.

Well, I might have just as well built a river raft and swung down along the Mississippi right beside Huck Finn and Jim and Tom Sawyer the way I felt leaning against the oak tree that autumn. I was the center, blowing pretend smoke from my pretend pipe, easing down onto the ground as the geese in the distant swamp called out beyond the dry reeds.

We are a nation in distress: we lie to each other in advertising campaigns, the Republican party lies about its intentions for the nation. The Democratic party lies about its intentions for the nation. We have a history of presidents who are lonely, confused, and insecure. We are a nation adrift, depending on self-appointed moralists for guidance, seeking advice from the Federal Reserve Board, being tricked each day by the media into believing that they have all the news.

We've done a good job tearing down just about everything from democratic principles to the author of *The Catcher in the Rye*. Can't we just all forgive each other, take a stick and poke the center to release the steam and begin again?

The woods are burning. Russia is on the brink of reverting back to a dictatorship. Women in our world are fare more vulnerable today than they have been in the past sixty years. The stock market defines imaginary boundaries of success. We have elections that have nothing to do with education, international food distribution, urban infrastructure, campaign reform, racism.

I remember being a boy in autumn smoking my imaginary acorn pipe and feeling just fine about myself and the world, believing that someday I could quite possibly be president of the United States. I don't believe any longer that there are such things as acorns the size of footballs.

Henri Nouwen called for a unity of heart within the historical and spiritual limits we humans struggle with on a daily basis. We can trace the beginnings of our own journey somewhere back in the days when acorn pipes were important.

When we put aside the ways of the child, we also put aside, too often, a purity of heart that was in the child. Henri Nouwen was a great man, not because of his writing or because of his personality or because of his charismatic appeal. He was a great man because he reminded us in a profound way what it is like to be children of God. Henri clearly defined the struggle we endure in our journey as we try and be our human and spiritual selves.

Are we mere cartoons of the spirit, wiggling through our daily routines in the failure of measuring up to what God intended, or are we whole figures, refined in our development as physical beings walking forward through the mist of life, seeing bits of salvation up ahead as we cling to each other in celebration of that hope?

It does not take a child very long to be involved with the imagination, to imagine something wonderful, to be stirred up inside and to greet the day or the pirate woods with an acorn pipe hanging from his lips as sails from the oak tree fling out above the mast against a steady wind. Boys can imagine such a ship. I can imagine, still, such a ship. Henri created a vision of God and a vision of self that makes the child in us remember a place where mud and wind and acorn and the voice of a sister were important and the elixirs of the day's passion. These are all hints of heaven.

This morning, as I looked out my window and watched that leaf fall, I wondered how much longer will my own journey be until I can return to the woods and to the ferns and to the days when my mother bakes bread and my father burned leaves in the yard and I, well, I whooped and ran out from the woods to show my father my acorn pipe.

We all struggle to return to the father. We long to return to the mother. When we find people along the way who are on the same journey, we feel a sense of relief and courage and ease. You see, Henri knew how to make terrific acorn pipes, and he'd feel just fine leaning back on the raft with Huck Finn and Jim and Tom Sawyer and with you and with me, and we'd just move along the journey of life, that river, that bleeding, tumultuous river out and down toward the sea.

Blow on the coal of the heart. Follow Job. We will all eventually be carried to the sea, to the first power, to the house of bread, to the power of a loving God waiting for our return. My mother said so. Henri Nouwen said so. God said so. Lord have mercy on us, Lord of the river, Lord of the sea, Lord of the journey, Lord of the acorn pipes.

Jubilate Deo.

Bibliography

The following list shows a selection of books currently in print by Henri Nouwen:

Behold the Beauty of the Lord: Praying with Jesus. Ave Maria, 1987.

Beyond the Mirror: Reflections on Death and Life. Crossroad, 1991.

Bread for the Journey: A Daybook of Wisdom and Faith. Harper-Collins, 1996.

Can You Drink the Cup? Ave Maria, 1996.

Creative Ministry. Doubleday, 1991.

A Cry for Mercy: Prayers from the Genesee. Doubleday, 1983.

The Genesee Diary: Report from a Trappist Monastery. Doubleday, 1981.

Gracias! A Latin American Journal. Orbis Books, 1993.

Heart Speaks to Heart: Three Prayers to Jesus. Ave Maria, 1989.

Here and Now: Living in the Spirit. Crossroad, 1994.

In Memoriam. Ave Maria, 1980.

In the Name of Jesus: Reflections on Christian Leadership. Crossroad, 1993.

The Inner Voice of Love: A Journey Through Anguish to Freedom. Doubleday, 1996.

Intimacy. HarperCollins, 1981.

Jesus and Mary: Finding Our Sacred Center. St. Anthony, 1993.

A Letter of Consolation. HarperCollins, 1990.

Letters to Marc about Jesus. HarperCollins, 1998.

Life of the Beloved: Spiritual Living in a Secular World. Crossroad, 1992.

Lifesigns: Intimacy, Fecundity, and Ecstasy in Christian Perspective. Doubleday, 1989.

Making All Things New: An Invitation to Life in the Spirit. Harper-Collins, 1981.

Ministry and Spirituality: Reaching Out, Creativity and Ministry. Continuum, 1996.

Our Greatest Gift: A Meditation on Dying and Caring. Harper-Collins, 1995.

Out of Solitude: Three Meditations on the Christian Life. Ave Maria, 1974.

The Path to Freedom. Crossroad, 1994.

The Path of Peace. Crossroad, 1994.

The Path of Power. Crossroad, 1994.

The Path of Waiting. Crossroad, 1994.

Reaching Out: The Three Movements of the Spiritual Life. Double-day, 1986.

Return of the Prodigal Son: A Story of Homecoming. Doubleday, 1994.

The Road to Daybreak: A Spiritual Journal. Doubleday, 1988.

The Road to Peace: Writings on Peace and Justice. Orbis Books, 1998.

Sabbatical Journey: The Final Year. Crossroad, 1989.

Show Me the Way: Reading for Each Day of Lent. Crossroad, 1994.

Thomas Merton: Contemplative Critic. Liguori, 1991.

Walk with Jesus: Stations of the Cross. Orbis Books, 1990.

The Way of the Heart: Desert Spirituality and Contemporary Ministry. HarperCollins, 1991.

With Burning Hearts: A Meditation on the Eucharist. Orbis Books, 1994.

With Open Hands. Ballantine, 1987.

The Wounded Healer: Ministry in Contemporary Society. Double-day, 1979.

Look for these books
by Christopher de Vinck

The Power of the Powerless

This is Christopher de Vinck's true account of his severely handicapped brother's life—a powerful, inspirational statement on the
value of life.

The Power of the Powerless is a doorway into the deep lessons of life,
love, and faith Christopher de Vinck learned from his brother Oliver.
It is a moving testimony to the power God demonstrates in the weakest of vessels. It poignantly affirms the immeasurable worth of every
person, and it attests powerfully to God's triumphant grace, which
transformed adversity into an altar of love and bound a family
together in a household of joy.

Softcover 0-310-48691-2

The Book of Moonlight

Weaving images and insight in prose and poetry, Christopher de Vinck helps us celebrate the seasons of life and see the hand of love and mercy in all our changing relationships. *The Book of Moonlight* is a reflection on the simple pleasures of love, marriage, family, community, and childhood—as charming and mysterious as moonlight glimpsed through the leaves of an ancient oak tree.

Hardcover 0-310-21255-3

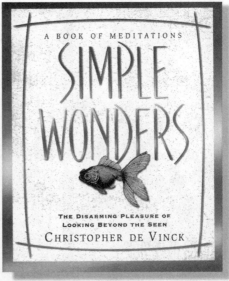

Simple Wonders:
The Disarming Pleasure of Looking Beyond the Seen

With his gifted writing style, de Vinck uncovers the truth and beauty in the ordinary in this book of daily meditations.

Simple Wonders offers glimpses into a complex and beautiful world, a world we often pass by in our busy lives. This is a world where daylilies glow a brilliant crayola orange, where the voice of God speaks to an old woman in a basket of knitting, and where ten-year-old boys and forty-year-old men discover wonder together in the jubilant details of creation.

This is a book for people who pray, for people who believe in God, and for people who want to enrich their lives by simply opening their eyes and looking at things in a different way. Placed in the context of the Bible, de Vinck's observations and stories about the small things in life—robins' eggs, children whispering, freshly-cut grass, a snake in a tree—illuminate universal truths and bring our griefs and our problems into a richer perspective.

Hardcover 0-310-49891-0

Threads of Paradise:
In the Fabric of Everyday Life

A follow-up to *Simple Wonders*, this book gives a different perspective on life, again helping us discover the truth and beauty in our ordinary, everyday lives.

This gifted writer, deftly using the power of language, helps us experience the wonder of a child's smile, a castle in the sand, a poet's heart, a mother's offering of freshly baked spice cake—and to see them as signs of Christ's eternal love speaking through common clay.

Offering a lyrical look at the fabric of our lives—the jumbled threads and tangled moments that seem to have no pattern—the author uses the small and finite to open the mind to a world of larger ideals. A cricket's song, a wheel of white cheese, worn stone steps, a jaunty straw hat, the giggle of a little girl, the splash of a small boy playing in a creek, the morning sun lighting the eastern horizon—through these de Vinck reminds us that golden threads shine among the dark on the tapestry of life.

Hardcover 0-310-49931-3

We want to hear from you. Please send your comments about this
book to us in care of the address below. Thank you.

ZondervanPublishingHouse
Grand Rapids, Michigan 49530
http://www.zondervan.com